Treasures for Scholars Worldwide

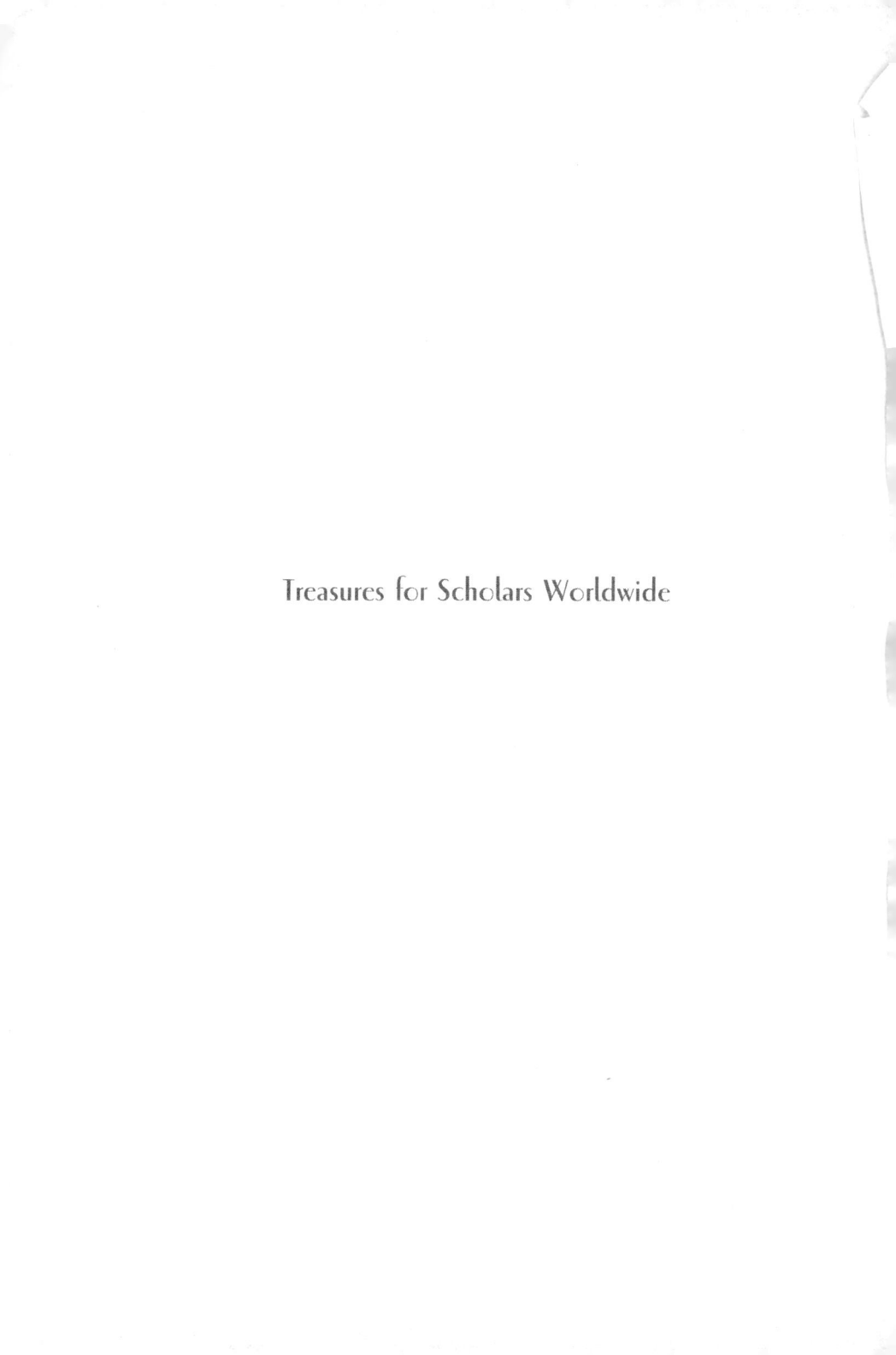

古籍保护丛书·姚伯岳 主编

Dictionary for Pest Control of Collections

藏品虫害防治词典

英汉对照

郭晓光 周华华 张国庆 韩丽伟 编著

广西师范大学出版社
GUANGXI NORMAL UNIVERSITY PRESS
·桂林·

藏品虫害防治词典
CANGPIN CHONGHAI FANGZHI CIDIAN

项目统筹　鲁朝阳
责任编辑　尚玉清
责任校对　金霖林
责任技编　王增元
书籍设计　徐俊霞　俸萍利 [广大迅风艺术]

图书在版编目（CIP）数据

藏品虫害防治词典：英汉对照 / 郭晓光等编著. —— 桂林：广西师范大学出版社，2024.8. —— （古籍保护丛书 / 姚伯岳主编）. —— ISBN 978-7-5598-7101-5

Ⅰ.G264.2-61

中国国家版本馆 CIP 数据核字第 2024AE6027 号

广西师范大学出版社出版发行

（广西桂林市五里店路 9 号　邮政编码：541004
　网址：http://www.bbtpress.com ）
出版人：黄轩庄
全国新华书店经销
广西昭泰子隆彩印有限责任公司印刷
（南宁市友爱南路 39 号　邮政编码：530001）
开本：880 mm ×1 240 mm　1/32
印张：7　　　　　　　字数：148 千
2024 年 8 月第 1 版　　2024 年 8 月第 1 次印刷
定价：88.00 元

如发现印装质量问题，影响阅读，请与出版社发行部门联系调换。

目录

前言 ·················· 1

正文

A	······ 1	N	······ 74
B	······ 10	O	······ 78
C	······ 15	P	······ 82
D	······ 26	Q	······ 93
E	······ 33	R	······ 94
F	······ 37	S	······ 99
G	······ 43	T	······ 108
H	······ 46	U	······ 112
I	······ 51	V	······ 113
J	······ 58	W	······ 116
K	······ 59	X	······ 120
L	······ 60	Y	······ 121
M	······ 65	Z	······ 122

附录一　常见馆藏害虫虫名检索 ………… *123*
　　（一）中文俗名检索 ……………………… *123*
　　（二）英文俗名检索 ……………………… *141*
　　（三）拉丁文学名检索 …………………… *159*
附录二　相关专业词汇 ……………………… *176*
附录三　不同藏品的虫害及其消杀法 ……… *206*
参考文献 ……………………………………… *214*

前　言

　　《藏品虫害防治词典（英汉对照）》是一部与危害藏品的昆虫相关的词典，共收录有2479个词条，内容涵盖昆虫名、藏品类型、虫害的防治方式等。其中有249个词条是昆虫名，其余多为与虫害防治相关的词条。所有词条均以英汉对照的方式列出，昆虫名还含有其拉丁文学名。本词典适于以下读者使用：博物馆、图书馆、档案馆等藏品管理单位，设有藏品保护等相关专业的高等院校，研究藏品保护的科研机构，以及从事仓储害虫管控的其他单位。

　　本词典由天津森罗科技股份有限公司的郭晓光、周华华、韩丽伟以及故宫博物院的张国庆等编写，复旦大学生命科学学院钟江教授审校。该词典中的词条大多是从相关的英文文献中直接摘录的，以便其能更好地成为藏品虫害治理研究的全球性交流工具。为了保证词义的准确性，编写者曾多次使用国际学术论文的相关词义对该词典进行检测与再审核。

　　本词典分为两大部分：正文与附录。正文部分为本词典词条的英汉对照，以英文词条的首字母检索对应的中文词义。附录分为三个部分，即常见馆藏害虫虫名检索（附录一）、相关专业词汇（附录二）以及不同藏品的虫害及其消杀法（附录三）。

　　附录一"常见馆藏害虫虫名检索"是为了便于查找昆虫名而设置的检

索工具，它有三种检索途径，即中文俗名检索、英文俗名检索及拉丁文学名检索。"中文俗名检索"是按照昆虫中文俗名的第一个字的拼音字母查找，可检索到该虫的英文俗名与拉丁文学名。"英文俗名检索"是按照昆虫英文俗名的第一个英文字母查找，可检索到该虫的拉丁文学名与中文俗名。"拉丁文学名检索"是按照该昆虫的拉丁文学名的第一个拉丁字母查找，可检索到该虫的英文俗名与中文俗名。

附录二"相关专业词汇"是对与虫害防治相关的专业词语的解释，这些专业词语编译自五份相关的英文文献，以英文单词的首字母排列检索。

附录三"不同藏品的虫害及其消杀法"是对国外一项研究的翻译，分别介绍了不同类型藏品可能面临的虫害，以及虫害发生后的消杀方式。

藏品虫害防治涉及的专业相当多，尽管编写组在编撰过程中十分谨慎，但难免有不当之处。敬请读者不吝赐教，以便今后的修订。

《藏品虫害防治词典（英汉对照）》编写组
2023年10月

A

Absorbency 吸收性

Absorption of moisture 吸湿，吸潮

Acanthoscelides 三齿豆象属

Accelerated deterioration 加速老化；加速劣化

Acid corrosion 酸腐蚀

Acid free tissue 无酸纸

Acid-free and lignin-free material 无酸及无木素的材料

Acidic component 酸性组分

Acidic compound 酸性化合物

Action against pests 防治虫害

Action threshold 行动阈值

Activate dormant spores 激活休眠孢子

Activated charcoal 活性炭

Activated silica gel 活化硅胶；活性硅胶

Active conservation 主动保护

Active humidity controller 湿度主动控制器

Active infestation 主动侵扰

Active insect infestation 活虫侵扰

Active insect population 活虫群体

Active mold 有活性的霉菌

Active mould spore 有活性的霉菌孢子

Active mycelium 活性菌丝

Active pest infestation 活虫侵扰

Active substance 活性物质；有效物质

Actively growing 生长活跃

Additional damage 额外损害

Additional treatment period 额外的处理时间

Adequate air circulation 充足的空气流通

Adherent moisture 附着水分

Adhesive 胶粘剂

Adhesive insect trap 粘性捕虫器

Adhesive material 粘结材料；胶粘材料

Adhesive moisture 吸附水分；粘附水分

Adhesive paste 浆糊；粘合剂

Adhesive tape 胶带

Adsorption moisture 吸附水分

Adult beetle 成年甲虫

Adult insect 成年昆虫

Adult stage 成虫期

Advanced stage of development 发育的晚期

Adverse environment 恶劣环境

Aerial mycelium 气生菌丝体；气中菌丝体；升空型菌丝

Aerosol atomizer 气溶胶喷雾器

Aerosol bomb 喷雾杀虫剂

Aerosol bombing 气溶胶喷射

Aerosol formulation 气溶胶配方

Aerosol spray 气溶胶喷雾剂

Affected item 受影响的藏品

Against moisture 防潮

Aged deterioration 老化变质

Aggregation pheromone 聚集信息素

Aging characteristic 老化特性

Air chamber 气腔空气包；空气室

Air circulation 空气循环；空气环流

Air conditioner 空调

Air conditioning vent 空调通风口，空调出风口

Air dehumidification 空气除湿

Air diffuser 风口

Air duct 进气道，风管，通风道

Air filter 空气过滤器

Air filter chamber 空气过滤室

Air intake 进气口

Air moisture 空气湿度

Air movement 空气流通

Air tight 气密

Air velocity duct 管道风速

Airborne contaminant 空气污染物

Airborne fungi 空气真菌

Airborne spray 空气喷雾剂

Air-borne 空气传播

Air-intake system 进气系统

Airtight confinement container 密闭容器

Airtight environment 密封环境

Airtight seal 气密密封

Alarm system 警报系统

Alkaline buffer 碱性缓冲液

Alkaline solution 碱性溶液

Allergen 过敏原

All-purpose fire extinguisher 通用灭火器

Almond moth *Ephestia cautella* (Walker) 粉斑螟

Alphitobius 菌虫属

Alternating action of freezing and thawing 冻融交替作用

Alternative strategy 替换策略；选择性策略

Alum-rosin size 明矾松香施胶

Amorphous silica gel 无定形硅胶；非晶硅胶

Amount of moisture 含水量

Anaerobic life 厌氧生物

Anaerobic metabolism 无氧代谢

Anaerobic microbe 厌氧微生物

Anaerobic respiration 无氧呼吸

Ancient paper 古纸

Anhydrous condition 无水条件

Animal glue 动物胶

Animal pest 动物虫害

Animal skin 动物皮

Anobiidae 窃蠹科

Anodized aluminum shelving 阳极电镀铝架

Anoxia bag 低氧袋

Anoxia chamber volume 低氧室的容积

Anoxia condition 低氧条件

Anoxia environment 低氧环境

Anoxia environment with oxygen absorbers 使用脱氧剂而形成的低氧环境

Anoxic (oxygen-less) air 低氧空气

Anoxic approach 低氧法

Anoxic cell 厌氧菌，厌氧生物，乏氧细胞

Anoxic disinfestation 低氧杀虫

Anoxic disinfestation bag 低氧杀虫袋

Anoxic display method 低氧展示法

Anoxic encasement 低氧防护套，低氧包装

Anoxic fumigation 低氧熏蒸

Anoxic microenvironment 低氧微环境

Anoxic preservation 低氧保存

Anoxic preservation system 低氧保存系统

Anoxic state duration 低氧状态持续时间

Anoxic treatment 低氧处理

Anoxic treatment exploits 低氧处理运用

Anoxic zone 低氧区

Antenna 触角

Anthicidae 蚁形甲科

Anthrenus 圆皮蠹属

Anthribidae 长角象虫科

Anti-deterioration 防劣措施

Antifungal agent 抗真菌剂

Antique furniture 古董家具，古典家具，仿古家具

Antiseptic cleaner 杀菌清洁剂

Anti-woodworm treatment 防蛀处理

Apidae 蜜蜂科

Apparel 服装

Appearance 外观，外貌

Appropriate material 合适的材料

Aqueous treatment 水性处理，含水处理

Archeological iron 考古发掘的铁器

Archival material 档案材料

Archival-quality box 档案箱

Archive 档案；档案馆

Areas containing collection 收藏区

Area-wide infestation 区域感染

Argon anoxic procedure 氩气低氧处理

Argon (Ar) gas 氩气

Arsenic 砷

Art collection 艺术收藏品

Art material 美术材料

Art on paper 纸上艺术品

Artefact 人工制品，手工艺品

Artefact versus content preservation 人工制品与内容保护

Arthropod 节肢动物，节足动物

Arthropod pest 节肢动物害虫，节足动物害虫

Arthropod repellant 驱虫药

Artifact（尤指具有历史或文化价值的）人工制品

Artifact/handicraft 手工艺品

Artifact pollution 人为污染

Artificially aging 人工老化

Ascospore 囊孢子，子囊孢子

Asexual reproduction 无性繁殖

Asexual spore 无性孢子

Aspirator 抽吸器，吸引器；吸气器

Associated pest 有关害虫

At-risk item 高危物品

Atmospheric component 大气成分；大气颗粒物

Atmospheric ozone layer 大气臭氧层

Atmospheric pressure plasma 大气压等离子体

Attagenus 毛皮蠹属

Attract insects 吸引昆虫

Attractant 引诱剂

Automatic shutting device 自动关闭装置

Avoid pests 消除害虫（侵扰）

B

Bacteria 细菌

Bacterial spore 细菌芽胞（芽孢）

Bait 饵

Baited insecticide 诱饵杀虫剂，饵杀虫剂

Baked enamel steel shelving 烤漆钢架

Bark & wood damaging insect 树皮和木材的害虫

Bark beetle 树皮甲虫；小蠹虫

Barrier film 阻隔薄膜，阻隔膜

Basidiospore 担子孢子

Batch treatment 分批处理

Beetle frass 甲虫蛀屑

Beetle pupae 虫蛹

Below-ground-level storage area 地下存储区

Bendiocarb 恶虫威（杀虫剂）

Benefit and danger 益处及风险

Best practice 最佳实践

Binding 粘结

Bioactivity 生物活性

Bioaerosol 生物气溶胶

Biocidal 杀生的；杀生物的；杀虫的

Biocidal additive 杀虫添加剂

Biocidal treatment 灭菌处理

Biocide 杀生物剂；杀虫剂

Biocide activity 杀生物活性

Biodegradation by insects 昆虫致生物降解

Biodeteriogen 生物致病原

Biodeterioration 生物危害；生物退化；生物变质；生物腐蚀

Biofilm 生物膜

Biogenic volatile organic compound 生物源挥发性有机化合物

Biohazard 生物危害

Biologic artifact 生物性人工产物；生物制品

Biological classification 生物学分类

Biological control 生物控制

Biological cycle 生物循环

Biological damage 生物损害

Biological deterioration 生物致劣化

Biological enemy 有害生物

Biological factor 生物学因素

Biological infestation 生物侵染

Biological method 生物学方法

Bioresmethrin 右旋反灭虫菊酯；生物苄呋菊酯（一种粮食保护剂、杀虫剂）

Bio-weathering 生物风化

Bird dropping 鸟粪

Biting insect 咀嚼口器害虫；咬虫

Bitten by insects 虫蛀

Blaberidae 折翅蠊科

Blast dehumidification 鼓风减湿

Blast freezer 送风冷柜，鼓风冷柜

Blattariae 蜚蠊目

Blattidae 蜚蠊科

Bleaching 漂白

Bleeding 渗色

Blotting paper 吸墨纸

Blunder trap 诱虫器

Book binding 书籍装订

Book copier 书籍复印机

Book pest control 图书病虫害防治

Book restoration 书籍修复

Borer activity 钻蛀虫活性

Borer hole 蛀孔

Borer population 虫数

Borer resistance 抗钻虫性

Borer/boring organism 钻孔生物

Boric acid 硼酸

Boring 穿孔，钻孔

Bostrychidae 长蠹科

Botanical 植物性药物

Botany specimen 植物标本

Bottled nitrogen 瓶装氮气

Bound material 粘合材料

Braconidae 茧蜂科

Branching mycelium 分枝菌丝体

Breeding 繁殖

Breeding activity 繁殖活动

Breeding season 繁殖季节；繁殖期

Bristles 刚毛

Broad-spectrum pesticide 广谱杀虫剂

Bruchidae 豆象科

Bruchidius 多型豆象属

Bruchus 豆象属

Brush wetting 刷洗

Bubble 透明罩

Buffering material 缓冲材料

Building crack and crevice 建筑物裂缝和缝隙

Building envelope 建筑围护结构

Building maintenance 建筑维护

Building perforation 建筑物裂口

Building sealing 密封建筑物

Building structure 建筑结构

Bulb duster 球形喷粉机

Buprestidae 吉丁科

Burrowing 掘穴，掘洞

C

Calcium carbonate 碳酸钙

Calcium chloride 氯化钙

Calcium sulfate 硫酸钙

Callosobruchus 瘤背豆象属

Camphor 樟脑

Cannibalistic 同类相食的，自相残杀的

Carabidae 步甲科

Carbamate 氨基甲酸酯

Carbamate-based pesticide 氨基甲酸酯类农药

Carbon dioxide fumigation 二氧化碳熏蒸

Carbon dioxide treatment 二氧化碳处理

Carcinogenicity 致癌性

Carcinogen 致癌物

Cardboard box 纸板箱

Cardboard glue-board 纸板胶合板

Carnivore 食肉动物

Carpenter ant 木匠蚁；木蚁

Carpenter glue 木工胶

Carpet beetle dermatitis 地毯甲虫皮炎

Carpophilus 果实露尾甲属

Caryedon 短颊粗腿豆象属

Case 套子，壳

Casing 蛹壳

Cast-off larvae skin 蜕掉的幼虫皮

Cast-off skin of the larva 幼虫脱落的皮

Cast skin 蜕皮

Caulking 填缝

Cause damage 造成危害

Cedar oil 香柏油

Cedar wood chest 香柏木木箱

Cellulose 纤维素

Cellulose degrader 纤维素降解剂

Cellulose material 纤维素材料

Cellulose molecule 纤维素分子

Cellulose synthase 纤维素合成酶

Cellulosic 纤维质的；纤维素质

Cellulosic enzyme 纤维素酶

Cellulosic fiber 纤维素纤维

Cellulosic textile 纤维纺织品

Central dehumidification system 集中除湿系统；集中空气干燥系统

Cerambycidae 天牛科

Cercus 尾须

Cerylonidae 拟坚甲科

Chalcididae 小蜂科

Chamber 腔室

Chamber fumigation 室内熏蒸

Characteristic damage 特征性损害

Check for leaks 检查泄露

Chemical 化学品

Chemical agent 化学试剂

Chemical biocide 化学杀灭剂，化学杀虫剂

Chemical bond 化学键

Chemical control 化学控制

Chemical decontamination 化学净化

Chemical disinfectant 化学消毒剂

Chemical fumigant 化学熏蒸剂

Chemical inertness 化学惰性

Chemical messenger 化学信使；有关细胞间化学讯息

Chemical method 化学法

Chemical pesticide 化学农药；化学杀虫剂

Chemical release agent 化学释放剂

Chemical stability 化学稳定性

Chemical treatment 化学处理

Chemically inert 不起化学作用的；化学惰性的

Chest freezer 柜式冷冻柜

Chest-type/household freezer 家用柜式冰箱

Chew hole 嚼噬洞

Chew through 咀嚼穿透，啃穿

Chewing insect 咀嚼式口器害虫

Chewing mark 咀嚼痕迹

Chewing mouthpart 咀嚼式口器

Chinese ink 中国墨

Chlorpyrifos 氯吡硫磷；毒死蜱

Chrome-plated steel shelving 镀铬钢架

Ciidae 木蕈甲科

Classification of insect 昆虫分类

Clean artifact 清洁人工制品；清洁藏品

Clean room 无尘室

Clean the collection 清洁馆藏

Clean-up effort 清理工作

Cleaning agent 清洁剂

Cleaning conservation 清洁养护

Cleaning method 清洗方式，清洗方法，清理方法

Cleaning procedure 清洁过程

Cleaning screen 清洗筛

Cleaning solution 清洗液

Cleridae 郭公虫科

Climate control for archive 档案馆气候控制

Climatic parameter 气候参数

Close vacuuming 紧密吸尘

Closed cabinet 封闭式柜架

Clothes moth （蛀蚀衣服等的）蠹虫；衣蛾

Clothes-moth proteinase 衣蠹蛋白酶

Clothes moth trap 衣蛾陷阱

Clutter-free 不杂乱的

Coated paper 涂布纸；铜版纸

Cockroach 蟑螂

Cocoon 茧

Cold cross-tolerance 冷交叉耐受性

Cold fogging concentrate 浓缩冷雾剂

Coleoptera 鞘翅目

Coleopterous insect 鞘翅目昆虫

Collect insects 收集昆虫

Collection 收藏品，馆藏

Collection area 藏品所在区域

Collection care 馆藏养护

Collection documentation 藏品文档

Collection or material type 藏品或材料的类型

Collection pest control 馆藏害虫控制

Collection room 珍藏室

Collection storage area 藏品库区

Collector stamp/mark 藏书印

Collembola 弹尾目；弹尾纲；弹尾类

Colony 菌落

Colony number 菌落总数

Color change 颜色变化，变色

Colored frass/excrement 彩色排泄物

Colydiidae 坚甲科

Comfort zone 适宜区域

Commercial freezer 商用冷柜

Common museum pest 常见的博物馆害虫

Common name of insect 昆虫俗名

Common pesticide application method 常用杀虫剂的施用方法

Common species 常见的种类

Common type 常见类型

Complete destruction 彻底损坏，完全毁灭

Complete sterilization 完全杀菌

Composite cellulose material 纤维素复合材料

Composite organic/inorganic item 有机/无机复合材料

Concentrated monitoring 集中监控，重点监控

Concentrated pesticide 浓缩的农药

Condensation 凝结

Conductive element 传导因素

Conidial fructification 产孢结构，分生孢子产孢结构

Conidium 分生孢子

Conservation activity 保护活动

Conservation application 保护应用方案

Conservation practice 养护实践

Conservation profession 保护专业

Conservation science 保护科学

Conservation technique 保护技术

Conservation treatment 保护治理

Constant hypoxia (CH) 持续低氧

Constant temperature 恒温，恒定的温度

Construction timber 建筑木材

Contact insecticide 触杀剂

Contact/residual spray 接触型/滞留喷雾剂

Contaminating agent 污染剂

Contamination 污染；污染物

Continue monitoring 持续监控

Control action 控制措施

Control insect infestation 控制虫害

Control insects 控制害虫

Control measure/method 防治方法，防控措施，控制方法

Control pests 控制虫害

Control strategy 控制策略

Control treatment 控制措施

Controlled atmosphere 气调

Controlled atmosphere technology 大气控制技术，气调技术

Controlled freezing 冰温，冷冻

Controlled heating 可控加热

Controlled low temperature treatment 可控低温处理

Controlled-temperature and humidity freezer 温湿度冷柜

Conventional chemical fumigation 常规/传统化学熏蒸

Conventional pest control 常规病虫害防治

Cool and ventilated space 阴凉通风处

Cool area 阴凉区域

Cool environment 阴凉环境

Corrode 腐蚀，侵蚀

Count insects 统计昆虫数

Crack 裂缝，裂隙；板间间隙

Crack-and-crevice treatment 裂缝与缝隙处理

Cracking 龟裂，破裂

Craquelure 龟裂痕，裂纹

Crawling insect 爬行的昆虫

Crawling larval insect 爬行的幼虫

Crevice 缝隙

Cricket 蟋蟀

Crucial growth factor 关键生长因子

Crustacea 甲壳纲的；甲壳纲动物

Cryptolestes 扁谷盗属

Cryptophagidae 隐食甲科

Cryptophagus 隐食甲

C-shaped C 形的

Cultural artifact 文化产品

Cultural collection 文化藏品

Cultural control 文化控制

Cultural heritage 文化遗产

Cultural heritage collection 文化遗产藏品

Cultural heritage institution 文化遗产机构

Cultural heritage material 文化遗产材料

Cultural heritage organization 文化遗产组织

Cultural heritage pest 文化遗产害虫

Cultural management 文化管理

Cultural property 文化财产；文化遗产

Cumulative depolymerisation 累积性解聚

Cumulative effect 累积效应

Curculionidae 象甲科

Cyclic defrosting freezer 循环式除霜冰柜

Cyladidae 蚁象甲科

D

D phenothrin 右旋苯醚菊酯

Damage and deterioration 损坏变质

Damage stage 危害的时期，危害的阶段

Damage to object 物品损坏

Damage to textile 纺织品损坏

Damaged by insects 虫损；虫蛀

Damaged page 损坏的页面

Damaged pointing 受损的勾缝

Damaging effect 破坏作用

Damaging environment 损坏的环境，破坏性环境

Damaging mold 有害霉菌

Damp and mould indicator 潮湿与霉菌指示器

Damp area 潮湿的地方

Damp basement 潮湿的地下室

Damp condition 潮湿情况

Damp flooring 潮湿的地板

Damp indicator 湿度指示器

Damp item 潮湿物品

Damp paper 潮湿的纸张

Damp room 潮湿的房间

Damp wood 潮湿的木材

Damper 风门

Damper actuator 风阀执行器

Data logger 数据记录仪

Deacidification 脱酸

Deacidification treatment 脱酸处理

Deactivate the mould 灭活霉菌

Deactivation 灭活作用

Dead insect 死虫，昆虫尸体

Dead insect debris 死虫残骸

Dead pest 死虫

Dead space 死腔；死区

Deal with contamination 处理污染

Debris 碎片，残骸

Decay 腐朽

Decision-making process 决策过程

Decontaminate 纯化，净化；去污，清洁；消毒

Decrease fading rates 降低褪色率

Deep clean 深度清洁

Deep freezing 低温冻结；深度冷冻（深冻）

Deeply ingrained dirt 陈积的污垢

Deep-seated mycelia 深层的菌丝

Degradation product 降解产物

Degree of deterioration 变质度；劣化度

Dehumidification blast 脱湿送风

Dehumidification drying 除湿干燥

Dehumidification drying kiln 除湿干燥室

Dehumidification of ventilation 通风干燥装置

Dehumidification system 干燥系统；去湿系统；去湿装置

Dehumidifier 除湿机

Dehumidify the space 对空间进行除湿

Dehydrate 脱水；去水

Deionized water 去离子水

Delicate object （不易保存的）易碎的物品

Dermaptera 革翅目

Dermestes 皮蠹属

Dermestid beetle 皮甲虫；皮蠹

Dermestidae 皮蠹科

Description of infestation 针对感染的说明

Desiccant 干燥剂；吸水材料；去湿的

Desiccant drying facility （含干燥剂的）干燥设备

Desiccated biological specimen 干燥的生物标本

Destroy the insects 消灭昆虫

Destructive pest 具有破坏性的害虫

Destructive phase 破坏性阶段

Detect 察觉；发现；探测

Deterioration 恶化，劣化；变质

Deterioration failure 变质失效；劣化失效；退化失效

Deterioration in storage 储存变质

Deterioration of protein 蛋白质变质；蛋白质恶化

Determine pest population 确定害虫数量/种群

Develop 发育；生长；进化；显露

Developing larvae 发育中的幼虫

Diatomaceous earth 硅藻土

Diazinon 二嗪磷，二嗪农，地亚农，敌匹硫磷

Dichlorodiphenyltrichloroethane (DDT) 二氯二苯基三氯乙烷；滴滴涕（杀虫剂）

Dichlorvos (vapona, DDVP) 敌敌畏

Different option of treatment 不同的处理方法

Digestive enzyme 消化酶

Digestive system 消化系统

Digital microscope 数字显微镜

Digital preservation 数字化保存

Digitization 数字化

Dimensional change 尺寸变化

Dinoderus 竹长蠹属

Direct spraying 直接喷洒

Direct sunlight 阳光直射

Dirt 脏污

Discolored 变色的；褪了色的；脱了色的

Discolored component 变色的部分

Discolouration 变色

Discourage insect attack 抑制昆虫的侵害

Disinfectant 消毒剂

Disinfecting solution 消毒液

Disinfector 灭菌器；消毒剂

Disinfest 消灭害虫，驱除害虫

Disinfest activity 杀菌活性

Disinfestant 除虫剂

Disinfestation 灭虫

Disinfestation effect 灭虫效果

Display 陈列

Display case 展示柜

Display material 展示材料

Distilled water 蒸馏水

Distribution map of pests 害虫分布图

DNA sampling DNA 采样

Document the findings 记录结果

Door sweep 门扫；门底密封条

Dormant 休眠的

Dormant mold 休眠的霉菌

Dormant (inactive) spore 休眠（非活性）孢子

Dormant state 休眠状态

Double bagging 双套袋；双层袋包装

Downy mildew 霜霉病；霜霉菌

Drafty/Draughty 通风良好的；通风的

Drain 排水沟

Dried botanical specimen 干燥的植物标本

Dried wood 干木

Droppings 鸟兽的粪便

Dry environment 干燥的环境

Dry rot fungus (*Merulius lacrymans*) 干腐菌

Dry sponge 干燥的海绵

Dry spore 干孢子

Dry timber borer 干木蛀虫

Duct tape 管道胶带；布基胶带

Dust（杀虫）粉剂

Dust cover 防尘罩

Dusting 喷药粉

Dynamic system 动态系统

E

Early warning 早期预警

Ecosystem approach 生态系统方法

Egg case 卵鞘

Egg sac 卵囊

Egg stage 卵期

Elevated temperature 高温

Elevator shaft 电梯井

Eliminate mold 消除霉菌

Eliminate the pest 消除有害生物；消除害虫

Elytra wing 鞘翅

Elytron 翅鞘

Embrittlement 脆化，脆裂

Emergence hole 羽化孔

Emergency planning 应急预案

Emerging adult 羽化成虫

Emulsifiable concentrate 乳油；浓缩乳剂

Emulsifying agent 乳化剂

Enamel-coated shelf 搪瓷货架

Encasement 装箱；包装物；外壳；使用包装套

Enclosure 装具

Endomychidae 伪瓢虫科

Entomologist 昆虫学家

Environmental condition 环境条件

Environmental control 环境控制

Environmental factor 环境因素

Environmental friendly 环保；环境友好的

Environmental monitoring 环境监测；环境监控

Enzymatic degradation 酶降解

Enzyme 酶

Enzyme treatment 酶处理

Equilibrium moisture content (EMC) 平衡含水率

Eradicate insects 消灭昆虫

Eradicate pests 消除害虫

Eradicate the infestation 消除（有害生物的）侵扰

Eradication procedure 消杀程序，消杀过程

Erotylidae 大蕈甲科

Escape door 逃生门

Essential oil 香精油

Establish colonies 筑巢

Etch 浸蚀；腐蚀剂

Ethics 伦理学

Ethylene oxide (ETO) 环氧乙烷

Ethylene oxide sterilizer 环氧乙烷消毒器

Eugenol 丁香酚

Eulan CN 防蠹磺

Eupelmidae 旋小蜂科

Even level 均匀度

Evidence of an infestation 虫害的迹象，虫害的证据

Evidence of pest 害虫痕迹

Example of insect 昆虫标本

Excessive handling 过度处理

Exclusion 杜绝；驱赶

Excrement 粪便，排泄物

Excreted residue 排泄物残渣

Excretion 排泄物

Exhibit area 陈列区

Exhibit case 展柜

Exhibition room 展示厅

Exit hole （虫）洞口；出口孔

Extent of the infestation 被侵害的程度

Exterior lighting 外部照明

Exterior structural wall 外部结构墙

Exterminate insects 消灭昆虫

External door 外门

Extraneous moisture 外部水分

Extreme temperature 极端温度

Extremely high moisture content 高湿

Extremely resistant 极强的抵抗力；极其顽固

Extremely toxic 剧毒

F

Fabric pest 织物害虫

Faecal pellet 粪便颗粒，虫屎颗粒

Faeces 粪便，虫屎

Family Dermestidae 家庭皮蠹科

Family Tineidae 家庭谷蛾科

Feather 羽毛

Fecal matter 粪便物

Fecal pellet 粪便颗粒

Fecal spot 虫屎的斑点

Fecundity 繁殖能力

Feeding 取食

Feeding behavior 觅食行为

Feeding damage 啃食损坏

Feeding debris　啃食碎屑

Feeding habit　食性

Feeding habit and trace　啃食习惯及痕迹

Feeding hole　啃食孔洞

Felt　毛毡

Female beetle　雌性甲虫

Fibre brittle　纤维脆化

Filamentous hyphae structure　丝状的菌丝结构

Filter　过滤器

Fine-mesh screen　细筛；精选机；精细筛网

Fine screen　细纱窗；细滤网；细筛；精筛

Finishing treatment　精细处理

Fire-proof storage　防火存储

Fissure　裂缝

Fix nitrogen　固定氮

Flathead borer　吉丁虫

Flea bomb　跳蚤炸弹

Floor drain　地漏

Fluctuating humidity　湿度波动

Flushing with nitrogen　氮气冲洗

Flying insect 飞虫

Fly-killing device 灭飞虫装置

Flyspeck 蝇粪留下的污点；污点

Fogging 雾化

Fogging of pesticide 雾化杀虫剂

Food attractant 食物引诱剂，食诱剂

Food residue 食物残渣

Food source 食物来源

Foraging pest 觅食的害虫

Formaldehyde 甲醛

Formaldehyde fumigation 甲醛熏蒸

Formicidae 蚁科

Fourier transform infrared (FTIR) spectroscopy 傅里叶变换红外光谱学

Fragile artefact 脆弱易损文物

Fragile material 脆弱易损材料

Fragile organic artefact 脆弱、易损有机制品

Frass 虫屑，蛀屑

Free coated tissue 自粘纸

Free moisture 游离水分

Freeze-dried animal specimen 冻干的动物标本

Freeze-drying 冷冻干燥

Freezer (upright and chest) 冷冻机（直立和柜式）

Freezer temperature 冷冻温度

Freezer treatment 冷冻处理

Freeze-thaw cycle 冻融循环

Freezing 冷冻

Freezing cycle 冻结的周期

Freezing environment 冷冻环境

Freezing object 冷冻对象

Freezing process 冻结过程

Freezing resistance 抗冻性，耐寒性

Freezing temperature 冻结温度

Freezing treatment 冷冻处理

Fresh exit hole 新的（虫噬）孔洞

Fresh frass 新鲜蛀屑

Friable media 脆弱、易损的媒介

Frost-resistance 抗冻性，耐寒性

Fruiting body 子实体

Full lifecycle 整个生命周期

Fully reversible 完全可逆

Fumigant 熏蒸剂

Fumigant gas 熏蒸气体

Fumigation 熏蒸

Fumigation agent 熏蒸剂

Fumigation bubble 熏蒸气泡

Fumigation insecticide 熏蒸杀虫剂

Fumigation machinery 熏烟机，熏蒸机

Fumigation plant 熏舱设备

Fumigation preparation 熏蒸制剂

Fumigation room 熏蒸室

Fumigation technique 熏蒸技术

Fumigation treatment 熏蒸处理

Fumigation using toxic chemicals 有毒化学熏蒸

Fumigation with toxic gases 有毒气体熏蒸

Fumigator 熏蒸机，熏蒸设备

Fungal activity 真菌活性

Fungal amylase 真菌淀粉酶

Fungal attack 霉菌侵袭

Fungal cell 真菌细胞

Fungal colony 真菌菌落

Fungal hyphae 真菌菌丝

Fungal infestation 真菌感染

Fungal mycelium 真菌菌丝体

Fungal outbreak 真菌爆发

Fungal particle 真菌粒子

Fungal spore 真菌孢子

Fungi 真菌

Fungicidal 杀菌的，杀霉的，杀真菌的

Fungicidal agent/Fungistat 抑菌剂

Fungicide 抑菌剂

Fungitoxic 毒害真菌的，对真菌有毒害性的

Fungitoxic effect 抗菌效应

Fungitoxicity 对真菌的毒性作用；杀真菌毒性；杀真菌效力

Fungus beetle 菌甲，真菌甲虫

Fuzzy 有茸毛的，覆着细毛的，绒毛状的

Fuzzy growth 绒毛状的生长

G

Gallery 虫道

Gamma irradiator γ 辐照器，伽马辐照器

Gamma radiation 伽玛辐射，伽马辐射，放射

Gap 缝隙

Gas fumigation 气体熏蒸

Gas phase 气态

Gas-proof 不透气的，气密的

Gas-proof sheeting 气密护板

Gas-tight structure 气密结构 / 不透气的结构

Gel bait 凝胶毒饵

Gelatinous material 凝胶状物质

General maintenance 日常维护

General pest 一般害虫

Germinate 萌发，萌动，萌芽

Germinating spore 萌芽孢子

Get mildew 发霉

Gibbium 裸蛛甲属

Glazed paper 上光纸/蜡光纸

Glue 各种胶粘物

Glue board 胶板；粘鼠板

Gnathocerus 角谷盗属

Gnaw 咬，啃，啮

Gnawing animal 啮齿动物

Gnawing mark 咬痕

Granular bait 颗粒状诱饵

Grazing 掠食

Green timber borer 生材蛀虫

Green to dry timber borer 生材到干材的蛀虫

Ground beetle 土鳖虫

Grub 幼虫，蛴螬（金龟甲等甲虫的幼虫）

Grub hole 虫孔

Grub-like 蛴螬状的

Gryllidae 蟋蟀科

Gutter 排水沟

H

Habit 习性

Habitat 动物栖息地

Hair 茸毛

Hand-duster 手工除尘器

Hand sheet 手工纸

Handling training 操作培训

Hanging trap 悬挂式陷阱，悬挂式诱虫器

Harbourage 躲藏处

Harborage site 藏匿处

Hard integument 坚硬的外皮

Hard-wall 硬壁

Hard wall chamber 硬壁室

Hardback book 精装书

Hardwood 硬木

Harmful insect 有害昆虫

Harmful organism 有害生物

Harmfulness 伤害，危害

Hatch 孵化

Heart-rot 心腐病

Heat and freezing treatment 冷热处理

Heat sealable 可热封的

Heat treatment 热处理

Heat treatment with moisture control 湿度可控的热处理

Heating 加热

Heating by microwave energy 微波加热

Heat-seal technique 热封技术

Heat-sealable plastic 热封塑料

Heat-set tissue 热接合纸

Heavy infestation 严重的侵扰

Helium gas 氦气

Hepa filter 高效过滤器，HEPA 过滤器

Hepa type filter 高效率微粒型滤网

Hepa vacuum 高效真空微粒吸尘器

Herbal specimen 植物标本

Herbaria collection 植物藏品

Herbarium specimen 腊叶标本

Herbivore 食草动物

Herbivorous insect 食草昆虫

Heritage 遗产；传统；文化遗产

Heritage building 文物建筑；古建筑

Heritage collection 文物收藏

Heterobostrychus 异翅长蠹属

Hide 兽皮

Hide glue 皮胶

Hiding place 隐藏的地方

High efficiency particulate air (HEPA) 高效空气过滤器

High-efficiency particulate air filter 高效微粒空气过滤器，HEPA 过滤器

High-filtration vacuum 高过滤真空吸尘

High heat 高热

High humidity source 高湿源

High hygienic standard 较高的卫生标准

High moisture wood 高含水量木材

High-risk collection 高风险藏品

High temperature 高温

High tolerance 高耐受性

Highly resistant 高耐受性

Highly resistant insect 高耐受性的昆虫

Highly susceptible 极易受影响的

Highly toxic 高毒性

Histeridae 阎虫科

Historic building 古建筑

Historic building component 历史建筑的构件

Historic collection 有历史意义的藏品

Historical document 历史文献

Hole 破洞，破孔；小孔

Holometabolic insect 全变态昆虫

Home freezer 家用冷柜

Horn 兽角

Host 寄主，宿主

Host material 基质材料，宿主材料

Host specificity 寄主专一性

Household pest 家居害虫

Housekeeping staff 库房管理人员

Human teratogen 人类致畸剂

Humid air 潮湿的空气，湿空气

Humidification 增湿

Humidifier 加湿器

Humidity requirement 湿度要求

HVAC 采暖、通风与空调系统，采暖通风与空调机电设备

HVAC system 暖通空调系统

Hydrogen cyanide 氰化氢

Hydrophobic/hydrophilic compound 疏水/亲水化合物

Hygrometer 湿度计

Hygroscopic 吸湿的

Hygroscopic material 吸湿性材料

Hymenoptera 膜翅目

Hypercapnic 碳酸过多的

Hypercarbia 高碳酸血症

Hyperoxia 高氧

Hypha 菌丝

Hypoxia 低氧，缺氧

I

Ideal moisture content 理想的水分含量

Identification 识别，鉴定

Identify insect damage 确定昆虫的危害

Identify mold 识别霉菌

Identify new pests 鉴别新的害虫

Identify pests 识别害虫

Identify pests and diagnose problem 识别病虫害并诊断问题

Image identification 识别（虫害）的图像

Immature insect 未成熟的昆虫

Immediate treatment 及时处理

Immersion method 浸泡法

Imperfect fungi 不完全菌；半知菌

Inactive mold 失去活性的霉菌

Incoming collection 入藏

Incubation temperature 孵化温度

Indicating desiccant 指示干燥剂

Indicator 指标

Indicator tablet 指示片剂

Indirect risk 间接性风险

Inert atmosphere fumigation 惰性气体熏蒸，惰性气氛熏蒸

Inert gas 惰性气体

Inert gas atmosphere 惰性气体气氛

Infected object 受感染的对象

Infection rate 感染率

Infest 骚扰；感染；寄生于

Infest softwood 寄生于软木

Infest with 侵扰

Infestation 有害生物大批出没，侵扰，蔓延；(昆虫)传染

Infestation of insect pests 虫害的感染

Infestation or suspected infestation 感染或疑似感染

Infestation spread 感染扩散

Infested artifact 被感染的人工制品

Infested material 被感染的材料

Infested object 被感染的物品

Ingest 咽下；摄取；吸收

Ingrained dirt 陈垢积污

Inhabit 栖息；居住于；占据

Inherent biological limitation 内在的生物局限性

Inherent characteristic 固有特性

Inherent resistance 内在抵抗力，固有抗性

Inhibit mold growth 抑制霉菌生长

In-house system 内部系统

In-house treatment 室内处理

Inlaid wooden object 镶嵌木制品

Inorganic barrier 无机屏障

Inorganic material 无机材料

Inorganic object 无机物品

Inorganic pesticide 无机农药

Inorganics 无机物

Insect activity 昆虫活动

Insect attack 虫害侵袭

Insect breeding 昆虫繁殖

Insect carcass 昆虫尸体

Insect cold hardiness 昆虫抗寒能力

Insect collection 昆虫馆藏

Insect damage 虫蛀，虫灾

Insect damage of wood 木材虫害

Insect debris 昆虫残骸

Insect dormancy 昆虫休眠

Insect droppings 昆虫粪便

Insect egg case 昆虫卵鞘

Insect families 昆虫科目

Insect gallery 昆虫展厅

Insect growth regulator 昆虫生长调节剂

Insect habitat 昆虫栖息地

Insect life cycle 昆虫生命周期

Insect monitor pad 昆虫监视器

Insect monitoring 昆虫监测

Insect mortality 昆虫死亡率

Insect order 昆虫目

Insect pest damage 虫害损害

Insect pest identification 害虫识别

Insect pest management 虫害管理

Insect pest monitoring 害虫监测

Insect pest of dry wood 干木害虫

Insect pest of moist wood 湿木害虫

Insect pest on wood 木材害虫

Insect pest traps monitoring form 捕虫器监测表

Insect population growth 昆虫种群繁殖

Insect-proof case 防虫箱

Insect repellent 驱虫剂

Insect resistance 防蛀性，抗虫性

Insect screen 防虫网

Insect specie 昆虫的种类

Insect-specific 昆虫特异性

Insect specimen 昆虫标本

Insect sticky 昆虫粘捕器

Insect sticky trap 昆虫黏性陷阱

Insect symbol 虫害的迹象

Insect taxonomy/Insect taxology 昆虫分类学

Insect trap 捕虫器

Insect waste 昆虫排泄物（蛀屑）

Insect-contaminated object 昆虫污染的物体

Insecticidal spray 杀虫喷雾剂

Insecticide 杀虫剂

Insecticide powder 杀虫粉

Insecticide safety 杀虫剂的安全性

Insecticide spray treatment 杀虫剂喷雾治理

Insects lay eggs 昆虫产卵

Inspection 检查

Inspection area 检查区

Inspection step 检查步骤

Inspection toolkit 检查工具包

Integrated control 综合控制

Integrated pest management (IPM) 病虫害综合防治

Integrated pest management for cultural heritage collections 文化遗产的虫害综合防治

Interaction of pesticides 杀虫剂的相互作用

Interceptor 拦截器

Intermittent hypoxia (IH) 间歇缺氧

Interventive conservation 干预性养护，介入性养护

Interventive treatment 干预性处理措施

Invasion 干预，介入

Invasive 侵害的

Invasive cleaning 有创清洁，侵入性清洗

Invasive technique 介入性技术

IPM tip 病虫害综合防治技巧

Irradiation 辐照

Irregular stain 不规则的污渍

Irreplaceable damage 无法补救的损害

Irreversible 不可逆的

Irreversible damage 不可逆的损害

Isolate affected material 隔离受影响的材料

Isolate artifacts 隔离藏品

Isolate objects 隔离对象

Isolate the problem area 隔离问题区域

Isolation period 隔离期

Isolation procedure 隔离程序

Isolation room 隔离室

Isopoda 等足目

Isoptera 等翅目

Isothiazolinone 异噻唑啉酮

J

Joinery 细木工制品

Juvenile hormone analog 保幼激素类似物

K

Keep pests out 防虫

Key location 关键位置

Key pest 重要害虫

Kill insects 杀虫

Kill rate 杀死率

Kinds of pests 害虫种类

Kytorhinus 细足豆象属

L

Labiduridae 蠼螋科

Lack of ventilation 缺少通风

Laemophloeidae 扁谷盗科

Languriidae 拟叩甲科

Large commercial freezer 大型商用冷冻柜

Large damage 重大损害

Large-pored hardwood 大孔隙硬木

Large scale treatment 大规模的处理

Larva 幼虫

Larval availability 幼虫存在性

Larval development 幼虫的发育

Larval instar 幼虫龄期，幼虫龄数

Larval molting 幼虫蜕皮

Larval skin 虫皮

Larval stage 幼虫期

Lathridiidae 薪甲科

Lavender oil 薰衣草油

Lay eggs 产卵

Leakage 泄露

Leather 皮革

Length of anoxic exposure 缺氧暴露时间

Length of treatment 处理的时间

Lepidoptera 鳞翅目

Lepidoptera insect 鳞翅目昆虫

Lepismatidae 衣鱼科

Lethal effect 致死作用，致死效应

Lethal high temperature 可致死高温

Library beetle 图书馆甲虫

Library collections conservation 图书馆馆藏保护

Life-cycle 生命周期

Life cycle of the pest 害虫的生命周期

Life cycle stage 生命周期阶段

Life expectancy 预期寿命

Life-safety measure （动物的）自我保护方式

Life span 寿命

Life stage 生命阶段

Light fixture 灯具固定架

Light-sensitive dye and pigment 光敏染料和颜料

Light shield 遮光罩

Light trap 光阱，光捕捉器

Lighting 照明

Lignin 木质素

Liposcelidae 书虱科

Liposcelis bostrychophila and other species of liposcelis (booklice) 嗜卷书虱和其他书虱物种（书虫）

Liquid stain 水渍

Live creature 活生物

Live on （动物）以……为食

Localized application of spray 局部喷洒喷雾剂

Localized approach 本地化措施

Localized condensation 局部冷凝

Localized humidity 局部湿度

Localized infestation 局部侵害

Localized treatment 局部处理

Long-term control measure 长期控制措施

Long-term stability 长期稳定性

Long-term storage 长期存放

Look for sign 寻找（虫害、霉菌）迹象

Loss of sheen 光泽损失

Low air circulation 低空气循环

Low hazard insecticidal spray 低危害杀虫喷雾

Low humidity 低湿度

Low moisture 低水分

Low oxygen atmosphere 低氧环境

Low oxygen controlled atmosphere 低氧气调

Low oxygen concentration 低氧浓度

Low oxygen fire prevention 低氧防火

Low-oxygen leakage rate 低氧泄漏率

Low-oxygen permeability 低氧渗透率，低透氧

Low oxygen treatment 低氧处理

Low-permeability 低渗透性

Low-permeability plastic bag 低渗透塑料袋

Low resistance 耐抗性低

Low risk 低风险

Low temperature 低温

Low-temperature storage 低温储存

Low-temperature treatment 低温处理

Low toxicity 低毒性

Lower humidity 较低的湿度

Lower the RH 降低相对湿度

Lure 诱饵

Lure board 诱饵板

Lyctidae 粉蠹科

M

Magnifying device 放大设备

Magnifying glass 放大镜

Major museum pest 博物馆主要害虫

Malathion 马拉硫磷

Marine borer 船蛀虫

Mass conservation 大规模保存

Mass conservation treatment 大规模的保护性措施

Mass treatment 大规模处理

Material type 材料类型

Mature colony 成熟的菌落

Mature larva 成熟的幼虫

Mature mold growth 成熟霉菌的生长

Mechanical cleaning 机械清洗

Mechanical control 机械控制

Megatoma 长皮蠹属

Mending 修补

Mending and filling technique 修补和填充技术

Merophysiidae 扁薪甲科

Metabolic product 代谢产物

Metal artefact 金属制品

Metal corrosion 金属腐蚀

Metal mesh 金属网

Metalized film 镀铝膜

Methyl bromide 溴甲烷；甲基溴；溴化甲烷

Methylated spirit 变性酒精；甲基化酒精

Mezium 茸毛蛛甲属

Micro-wave 微波

Microbial growth 微生物生长

Microbial volatile organic compounds (MVOCs) 微生物挥发性有机化合物

Microclimate 小微环境

Microclimate solution 小微环境解决方案

Microcrystalline 微晶（质）的

Microencapsulated insecticide 微囊杀虫剂

Microencapsulated pyrethrin 微胶囊除虫菊酯

Microfungi 微真菌

Microfungi attacking paper objects 侵害纸制品的微真菌

Microorganism 微生物

Microorganism growth 微生物生长

Microorganism symbol 微生物迹象

Microwave energy 微波能

Microwave heating 微波加热

Microwave modulator radiation 微波调制器辐射

Microwave radiation 微波辐射；微波射线；微波

Microwave radiation energy 微波辐射能量

Microwave thermal radiation 微波热辐射

Mild fumigant 药性温和的熏蒸剂

Mildew （使）发霉,（使）长霉

Mildew and rot 霉烂

Mildew attack 霉的侵袭；生霉，发霉

Mildew-growing 长霉

Mildew in textile 纺织物霉腐变色

Mildew inhibitor 防霉剂

Mildew proof 防霉的

Mildew resistance 抗霉性；防霉性

Mildew-retarding agent 防霉剂

Mildew spot 霉斑

Mildew stain 霉斑；霉点

Mildew stained 有霉渍点的

Mildewproof 防霉的

Mildewy odor 发霉的气味

Minimal intervention 最小干预

Minimal modified atmosphere 微气调

Minor blemish 微小瑕疵

Mishandling 错误处理，误操作

Misting 雾化

Mite 螨虫类

Mixed material 混合型资料，混合材料，混合材质

Mobile chamber 移动处理室

Moderately resistant insect 中等抗性昆虫

Modified atmosphere (MAS) 气调

Modified atmosphere CO_2 treatment 二氧化碳的气调处理

Modified atmosphere packing 气调包装

Modified atmosphere treatment 气调处理

Modified or controlled atmosphere treatment 气体调控处理

Modify climatic conditions 改变环境条件

Moist area 潮湿地区

Moisture 潮湿，湿气，水分

Moisture-conditioned nitrogen 经过湿度调节的氮气

Moisture content 含湿量，水分含量

Moisture-damaged wood 受潮损坏的木头

Moisture-loving pest 喜湿性害虫

Moisture meter 湿度计，湿度表

Moisture pest 潮虫

Moisture-sensitive 易潮的；湿敏性的

Moisture source 湿气源

Mold and mildew 霉菌和霉变

Mold contamination 霉菌污染

Mold damage 霉菌损害

Mold-damaged object 霉菌损坏的物品

Mold-damaged paper 霉菌损坏的纸张

Mold growth 霉菌生长

Mold infestation 霉菌感染

Mold infested object 受霉菌侵染的物体；发霉的物品

Mold mycelia 霉菌菌丝

Mold outbreak 霉菌爆发

Mold propagates 霉菌传播

Mold remediation 灭菌的补救

Mold removal 除霉

Mold removal archive 霉菌清除记录

Mold removal method 除霉方法

Mold spore 霉菌孢子

Moldy object 发霉物品

Molecular method 分子生物学方法

Molt 蜕皮

Monitoring and inspection 监督检查

Monitoring chart 监控图

Monitoring data 监测数据

Monitoring device 监控设备

Monitoring strategy 监控策略

Monitoring system 监控系统

Monitoring to detect insects 监测昆虫，监测以检测昆虫

Monitoring trap 监控陷阱

Monotomidae 球棒甲科

More delicate manner 更精细的处理

More tolerant insect 更具耐受性的昆虫

More tolerant towards humidity and temperature 对温湿度耐受性更强

Mortality probability 死亡概率

Mortality rate 死亡率

Mortality/survival ratio 死亡率/存活率

Mortally affected 致命影响

Most abundant pest specie 最多的害虫种类

Most active infestation 最活跃的虫害

Most damaging moth 最具破坏性的飞蛾

Most destructive 最具破坏性的

Most destructive food pest 最具破坏性的食品害虫

Most vulnerable collection 极易损的藏品

Moth 蛾类

Moth-eaten old cloth 蛀坏的旧衣物

Moth repellent 驱蛾剂

Mothball 防蛀球，卫生球

Mould 霉菌

Mould colony 霉菌菌落

Mould-contaminated object 受霉菌污染的物品

Mould-feeding beetle 以霉菌为食物的甲虫

Mould fragment 霉菌碎片

Mould growth 霉菌生长

Mould outbreak 霉菌爆发

Mould spore 霉菌孢子

Mould stain 霉斑

Mouldy and damp object 发霉和潮湿物品

Mouldy library material 发霉的图书馆资料

Mouldy or musty smell 陈腐的或发霉的气味

Moult 蜕皮；脱毛，换羽

Mouthpart 昆虫等的口器

Multiply 繁殖

Mummy 木乃伊

Museum application 博物馆的应用

Museum collection 博物馆藏品

Museum environment 博物馆环境

Museum housekeeping 博物馆的内务管理

Museum object 博物馆物品

Museum pest 博物馆害虫

Museum pest specie 博物馆害虫种类

Museum specimen 博物馆标本

Musty odor 发霉的气味

Musty smell 霉烂味

Mutagenicity 致突变性

Mycelia 菌丝

Mycelial cushion 菌丝层

Mycelial fungus 丝状真菌

Mycelial growth 菌丝生长，菌丝体生长

Mycelial phase 菌丝期；菌丝体相

Mycelial plaque 菌丝毡

Mycelial structure 菌丝结构

Mycelium 菌丝体

Mycetophagidae 小蕈甲科

Mylar 聚酯薄膜

N

Naphthalene 萘；臭樟脑

Natural animal fiber 天然动物纤维

Natural crystalline camphor 天然结晶的樟脑

Natural decay 自然腐烂，自然腐蚀；自然衰变，自然衰减

Natural habitat 自然栖息地，自然生态环境

Natural history specimen 天然形成的历史标本

Natural pyrethrin 天然除虫菊精

Natural resistance 自然抗性，先天抵抗力

Negative pressure fume hood 负压通风柜

Negatively affect 负面作用

Negligible damage 极其轻微的损坏

Nest/burrow 巢穴

Nesting 筑巢

Nesting material 筑巢材料

Network of tunnel 虫道网

New infestation 新的感染

Nitidula 露尾甲属

Nitidulidae 露尾甲科

Nitrogen anoxia 低氧氮气环境

Nitrogen anoxia treatment 低氧氮气处理

Nitrogen-based anoxic treatment 基于氮的低氧处理

Nitrogen cylinder 氮气瓶

Nitrogen flushing 吹氮

Nitrogen fumigation 氮气熏蒸

Nitrogen (N_2) gas 氮气

Nitrogen generator 制氮机

Nitrogenase 固氮酶

Non-chemical alternative 非化学替代法

Non-chemical control 非化学控制

Non-chemical method 非化学法

Non-chemical trap 非化学陷阱

Non-chemical treatment 非化学处理

Non-chemical vulcanized rubber sponge 非化学硫化橡胶海绵

Non-corroding wire mesh 抗腐蚀的金属丝网

Non-harmfulness 无害的

Non-invasive method 非侵袭方式

Non-pest 无害昆虫，非害虫

Non-pest insect 无害昆虫，非害虫

Non-pest organism 无害生物

Non-porous surface 无孔的表面

Non-specific 非特异性

Non-staining adhesive 不着色的粘合剂

Non-toxic 无毒性

Non-toxic anoxia pest control 无毒低氧害虫防治

Non-toxic control 无毒防治

Non-toxic eradication 无毒歼灭

Non-toxic fumigation 无毒熏蒸

Non-woven material 无纺布材料

Nonabrasive erasing material 非磨蚀性擦除材料

Nonfumigant insecticide 非熏蒸剂杀虫剂

Normal condition 正常条件

Noxious odor 有毒气体

Nutrient 营养物，营养素

Nymph 若虫

Nymph stage 若虫阶段

O

Object stained 被弄脏的物品

Object with inlays 具有镶嵌物的对象

Occasional invader 偶尔入侵者

Off-gas 废气，尾气；(新物品中的)残留挥发物

Off-gassing toxin 尾气的毒素；残留挥发物中的毒素

Oil-based formulation 油基配方

Oil concentrate insecticide 油浓缩杀虫剂

Oil concentrate 浓缩油

Oil of cloves 丁香油

Oil of red cedar 红雪松油；红杉油

Oil painting 油画

Old exit hole 旧孔洞

Old or non-active infestation 早期的或非活动性的虫害

Old paper 旧纸张（文献、报纸）

Omnivore 杂食动物

Omnivorous 杂食的，杂食性的，无所不吃的

Omnivorous group 杂食者

Omosita 窝胸露尾甲属

On-site nitrogen generation 现场制氮

Oospore 卵孢子

Oothecae 卵鞘

Open storage rack 开放式的存储架

Optimal growth condition 最佳生长条件

Optimal temperature 最佳温度，最适温度

Organic acid 有机酸

Organic collection 有机藏品

Organic dust 有机粉尘

Organic fibre 有机纤维

Organic glue 有机胶

Organic material 有机材料

Organic matter 有机质，有机物

Organic nutrient 有机营养物

Organic pesticide 有机农药

Organic pesticide spray 有机农药喷雾

Organic residue 有机残留物

Organism type 生物类型

Organoarsenic insecticide 有机砷杀虫剂

Organochloride insecticide 有机氯杀虫剂

Organophosphate 有机磷

Organophosphorous pesticide 有机磷农药，有机磷杀虫剂

Original artifact 原始物件

Original material 原始材料

Orphinus 球棒皮蠹属

Orthophenyl phenol 邻苯酚

Orthoptera 直翅目

Oryzaephilus 锯谷盗属

Outdoor environment 户外环境

Outer shell 外壳

Oval hole 椭圆形裂洞

Oxidation 氧化，氧化作用，氧化反应

Oxidative bleaching 氧化漂白

Oxygen absorber/scavenger 除氧剂，脱氧剂

Oxygen barrier film 隔氧膜

Oxygen burner system 氧气燃烧器系统

Oxygen deprivation 除氧，缺氧

Oxygen desorption time 氧脱附时间

Oxygen drop time 氧气下降的时间

Oxygen indicator 氧指示剂

Oxygen level 氧含量

Oxygen monitor 氧监测仪

Oxygen permeability 透氧性

Oxygen-rich air 富氧空气

Oxygen-rich environment 富氧环境

Oxygen scavenger treatment 除氧剂处理

Oxygen transmission rate (OTR) 氧气透过率

P

Packing material 包装材料

Painting on canvas 布面绘画

Painting support 绘画支架

Palorus 粉盗属

Pantry pest 储藏室害虫

Paper artifact 纸制品

Paper-based item 纸质品

Paper-based material 纸质材料

Paper-based storage material 纸质存储材料

Paper chemistry 造纸化学

Paper conservation 纸质品保存

Paper file 纸质档案

Paper's acidity 纸张的酸性

Paradichlorobenzene/P-dichloro-benzene (PDB) 对二氯苯

Paradicholoro-benzene crystal 对二氯苯晶体

Parasitoid wasp 寄生蜂

Parchment 羊皮纸

Passandridae 隐颚扁甲科

Passive conservation 被动式保护

Passive humidity buffering 湿度被动缓冲

Peak time 高峰时段

Pellet 粪球；干屎粒

Penetrating gas 渗透性气体

Perimeter invader 周边入侵（的有害生物）

Periodic assessment 定期评估

Periodical general cleaning 定期大扫除

Permanent damage 永久性损坏

Permethrin 氯菊酯

Persistent pesticide 残留性农药

Personal protective clothing 防护服

Personal protective equipment (PPE) 个人防护设备

Pest 害虫

Pest activity 害虫活动

Pest associated with mould and high humidity 与霉菌和高湿度有关的害虫

Pest attack 害虫侵袭

Pest beetles 甲虫类害虫

Pest biology 害虫生物学

Pest-conductive condition 害虫传播和扩散的条件

Pest control 害虫防治

Pest control inspection 害虫防治检查

Pest control staff 虫害防治人员

Pest damage 害虫危害

Pest description 害虫的描述

Pest entry 有害生物的进入

Pest excrement 害虫的排泄物

Pest food source 昆虫的食物来源

Pest-free environment 无虫的环境

Pest habitat 害虫栖息地

Pest incident 虫害事件

Pest infestation 虫害

Pest infestation site 害虫侵扰点

Pest intruder 入侵的害虫

Pest management 病虫害防治，害虫管理

Pest management technique 虫害防治技术

Pest monitoring program 害虫监测项目

Pest population 害虫种群

Pest present 害虫出现

Pest prevention 虫害预防

Pest prevention policy 虫害防治政策

Pest-proof container 防虫容器

Pest-proofing 防虫

Pest remain or trace 害虫残留物或痕迹

Pest repellent 驱虫剂

Pest resistance 抗虫性

Pest-resistant container 抗虫害的容器

Pest-resistant material 抗虫害的材料

Pest risk assessment 虫害风险评估

Pest specie 害虫种类

Pest strip 防虫条

Pest subtype 害虫亚型

Pest trace 害虫痕迹

Pest trap 害虫陷阱

Pest trapping program 害虫诱捕计划

Pest-vulnerable area 易受虫害影响的地区

Pest's biology 害虫生物学

Pest's habit 害虫习性

Pesticide 杀虫剂

Pesticide application 施用农药

Pesticide dust 杀虫粉剂

Pesticide fog 杀虫雾，农药雾

Pesticide formulation 农药剂型

Pesticide screening 杀虫剂筛查

Pesticide treatment 杀虫剂处理

Phemone trap 信息素诱捕器

Phenothrin 苯醚菊酯；苯氧司林；苯诺茨林

Pheromone 信息素

Pheromone lure 信息素诱剂

Pheromone lure trap 信息素诱捕陷阱

Pheromone trap 信息素陷阱

Pheromone trapping program 信息素诱捕程序

Phosphine 磷化氢，磷烷

Phradonoma 齿胫皮蠹属

Phyllodromiidae 姬蠊科

Physical barrier 物理屏障

Physical condition 实际条件；实际状态；物理状况

Physical distortion 物体变形

Physical injury 物理性损伤

Physical make-up 装帧

Physical method 物理法

Physical removal 物理去除

Physiological state 生理状况

Phytochemical 植物中的天然物质，植物化学物质

Picky eater 对食物挑剔的虫类

Picture frame 相框，框架，画框

Pigment 颜料，染料；色素

Pigment system 色素系统，色素体系

Pigmentation 色素淀积，着色（作用）

Plant based textile 植物性纺织品

Plant essential oil 植物精油

Plant fibre 植物纤维

Plant material 植物材料

Plasma 等离子体

Platypodidae 长小蠹科

Plywood 胶合板

Poison free method 无毒的方法

Poisoning 毒杀

Polyethylene bag 聚乙烯袋

Polymer backbone 共聚物主链

Poo 虫屎

Poor condition 恶劣条件

Poor damp proofing 防潮性能差

Poor environment 不良环境，恶劣的环境

Poor environmental condition 恶劣的环境条件

Poor handling 处理不当

Poor sanitation 卫生条件差

Poor ventilation 通风不良

Porous material 多孔材料

Portable dehumidifier 便携式除湿机

Potential application 潜在的应用

Potential entry point （有害生物）潜在的入口点

Potential insect pest species 潜在害虫的种类

Potential mold growth 潜在的霉菌生长

Powder-coated steel shelving 粉末涂层的钢架

Powder-post beetle 木蠹虫或粉蠹虫，鞘翅目长蠹总科粉蠹科的通称

Powdered iron oxide 氧化铁粉末

Powdery mildew 白粉病；白粉菌；粉霉病；白粉霉病

Precaution 预防措施

Preferential insect damage 虫害的首选（补救措施）

Presence indicator （虫害）迹象

Presence of frass 出现蛀屑

Preservation strategy 保存策略

Preservation survey 保护性检测；保护方面的调查，保存状况的检查

Pressure-sensitive (self-adhering) tape 压敏胶带

Pressurized hand sprayer 加压手动喷雾器

Prevent fungal growth 预防真菌生长

Prevent pest entry 防止害虫进入

Preventing pests 预防害虫

Prevention & remediation 预防和补救

Preventive care 预防性护理

Preventive maintenance 预防性维护

Preventive measure 预防措施

Preventive pest management 预防病虫害管理

Preventive technique 防治技术

Preventive treatment 预防性处理

Previously infested 曾经被感染的

Primary pest 主要害虫

Principal damage 主要危害

Printing ink 印墨

Prioritize preservation 优先保存

Priority 优先顺序，优先级别

Proactive maintenance 主动维护，积极地维护

Procreation 生殖，生育

Progressive damage 进行性破坏，渐进性损害

Proofing 防护

Proper temperature 适宜的温度

Propoxur 残杀威；安丹

Protective box 保护盒

Protective enclosure 保护性装具

Protein-based material 蛋白质基材料

Protein/proteinaceous material 蛋白质材料

Psocid 啮虫；啮虫科昆虫；书虱

Psocoptera 啮虫目

Ptinidae 蛛甲科

Ptinus 蛛甲属

Public area 公共场所

Pupa 虫蛹

Pupal case 蛹壳

Pupal cell 蛹体

Pupal chamber 蛹室

Pupal period 蛹期

Pupal sac 蛹囊

Pupal tube or case 蛹管或壳

Pupate/pupation 化蛹，蛹化

Purge rate（惰性气体）吹扫率

Purified water 净化水

Pyrethrin 除虫菊酯；拟除虫菊素

Pyrethrin residuce 菊酯农药残留

Pyrethroid 拟除虫菊酯

Pyrethroid fumigation 拟除虫菊酯熏蒸

Pyrethroid insecticide 拟除虫菊酯类杀虫剂

Pyrethroid pesticide 拟除虫菊酯类农药；菊酯类农药

Pyrethrum cineraefolium 除虫菊

Pyrethrum insecticide 除虫菊酯杀虫剂

Q

Quarantine area 检疫区

Quarantine room 隔离室

Quarantine rule 检疫规则

R

Radiation 辐射，放射物

Radical treatment 根治

Radio frequency energy 射频能量

Rapidly knock down insects 迅速消灭害虫

Rare book 珍本书

Rare textile 珍贵的织物

Reaction to pests 对害虫的反应

Reactivate 再活化，再激活

Reactive oxygen scavenger 活性氧清除剂

Record keeping 记录保存

Recover 恢复

Red rot 赤腐病

Redox reaction 氧化还原反应

Reduce pest conditions 减少生虫的条件

Reduction mechanism 还原机理

Reference species 参考物种

Reformatting techniques 重新格式化技术

Refrigeration-based dehumidifier 制冷除湿机

Regular checking 定期检查

Regular dusting 定期除尘

Regular exchange 定期更换

Regular thorough cleaning 定期彻底清洁

Rehabilitation works 修复工程

Reinfestation 再次蔓延

Relative humidity (RH) 相对湿度

Remedial conservation 补救性保护

Remedial measure 补救措施

Remedial works 补救工程，补救工作

Remediation of defects 缺陷修补

Remediation procedure 补救程序

Remove adhesive 去胶黏剂

Remove dust 除尘

Remove mould 清除霉菌

Remove pests safely 安全地清除害虫

Repair technique 修复技术

Repeat cooling 重复冷冻

Repel insects 驱除昆虫

Repellent 驱虫剂

Repellent effect 驱避作用

Repellent product 驱虫产品

Reproduce 繁殖

Reproduction ceases 繁殖停止

Reproduction in fungi 真菌繁殖

Reproductive process 繁殖过程

Reproductivity 繁殖能力

Residual and vapor pest strip 滞留和蒸气性杀虫条

Residual effect 后遗效应，残留效应

Residual insecticide/pesticide 滞留杀虫剂

Residual spray 滞留喷雾

Residue 残渣，残留物

Residue remain 滞留物

Resilient nature 抗御性

Resistance 抵抗力

Resistant insect 耐抗性昆虫

Resistant species 抗性强的（虫）类

Respond 做出反应；承担责任

Respond to infestation 应对侵扰

Restoration 修复，复原

Resurgence of pests 害虫回升

Return air vent 回风口

Reversible 可逆的

Reversible method 可逆的方法

Rhinotermitidae 鼻白蚁科

Right amount 适量

Risk zone 风险区

Rodent 啮齿动物，啮齿类

Rodent bait 啮齿动物诱饵

Rodent smudge mark 啮齿动物弄脏的痕迹

Roof penetration hole 屋顶渗透孔

Room temperature 室温

Root borer 钻蛀植物根茎的害虫（某些天牛、透翅蛾等的幼虫）

Round hole 圆孔

Route of entry 侵入途径

Routine inspection 例行检查

Routine maintenance 例行维护；日常维护

Rust-colored spot 铁锈色斑点

S

Safety equipment 安全设备

Salvage 抢救,救助

Sanitation 环境卫生

Sapwood 边材

Scavenger 食腐动物

Scientific evidence 科学证据

Scolytidae 小蠹科

Scraping 刮痕;刮屑,削刮的碎屑

Screening 筛查

Seal crack 密封裂缝

Seal opening 密封口

Seal the building 密封建筑物

Sealable enclosure 可密封外壳

Sealed box 密封盒

Sealed collections room 密封的收藏室

Sealed oxygen-free environment 密封的无氧环境

Sealed plastic bag 密封塑料袋

Sealed showcase 密封陈列柜

Sealed space 密封空间

Sealing barrier strip 密封条

Seasonal pattern 季节性（行为）模式

Secondary infestation 继发性侵扰

Secondary pest 次要害虫

Secure storage 安全存储

Seed viability 种子活力，种子活性

Selective nutrient 选择性养分

Selective temperature 可选温度

Self-closing device 自动关闭装置

Self defrost freezer 自动除霜冰柜

Self-destruct （引起）自毁的

Self-dispensing container 自分配容器

Semiochemical 化学信息素

Sensitive material 敏感材料

Sensitive media 敏感性介质

Sensitive metal 敏感金属

Separate treatment 单独处理

Serious damage 严重伤害，严重损坏

Serious insect infestation 严重的昆虫侵扰

Setting out the traps 设置陷阱，设置捕虫器

Sex pheromone 性信息素

Shed skin 蜕皮

Shelf life 保质期

Shelter 藏匿处，掩蔽处

Short-lived insect 寿命较短的昆虫

Short-term control measure 短期控制措施

Shot hole pin hole 小虫孔

Shot-hole 穿孔，虫孔

Shred 咬成碎片

Side effect 副作用

Sign of infestation 侵扰的迹象

Sign of pest activity 有害生物活动的迹象

Significant risk 重大风险

Silica gel 硅胶

Silica gel desiccant 硅胶干燥剂

Silvanidae 锯谷盗科

Silvanoprus 叶跗锯谷盗属

Simple sugar 单糖

Single-item treatment 单项处理

Sinoxylon 双棘长蠹属

Site-remediation project 现场补救项目

Size（用面粉、树胶、树脂等配制的）胶料、浆糊等

Skeleton specimen 骨骼标本

Skin 兽皮；皮革；皮制品

Slow development 发育缓慢

Slow eater 慢食者

Small dust-like colony 微尘状菌落

Small rodent 小啮齿动物

Small-scale air drying 小规模风干

Small stain 小污渍

Smell musty 有霉味

Smudge 污迹

Snap trap 捕捉器

Sodium vapor lighting 钠蒸汽灯

Soft-wall 软壁

Soft wall chamber 软壁室

Soft-walled enclosure system 软壁封闭系统，柔性封闭系统

Soft wood 软木

Soiled object 弄脏的东西

Soiled woolen 弄脏的毛织品

Soiling and staining 污染和污损

Solid media 固体介质

Solid state 固态

Solid-walled container system 刚性容器系统

Solution 解决方案

Solvent cleaning 溶剂清理

Space fogging 空间喷雾

Specialized equipment 专用设备

Specialized vacuum cleaner 专用真空吸尘器

Specific morphological character 特定的形态特征

Spin silk 吐丝

Sporadical high relative humidity 偶发较高相对湿度

Spore 孢子

Spore germination 孢子萌发

Spore sac 孢子囊

Spore viability 孢子的活力

Sporodermis 孢粉壁

Spray pesticide 喷雾杀虫剂

Sprayer 喷雾器

Spread the infestation 传播虫害

Spring-tide 全盛期

Springtail 弹尾目昆虫；跳虫

Stabilization 稳定化处理

Stagnant air （密闭空间内）静止的非流动空气

Stain migration 污渍迁移：污渍扩散；色素迁移

Stain paper 玷污纸张

Staining 染色；斑点

Standard 标准

Standing water 积水

Staphylinidae 隐翅虫科

Starch adhesive 淀粉粘合剂

Starch glue/paste 淀粉胶水，淀粉胶

Starch sizing 淀粉胶料

Starch-adhesive pasted paper 有淀粉粘合剂的糊纸

Starchy material 淀粉质材料

Static anoxia treatment 静态低氧处理

Static system 静态系统

Stem borer 钻心虫

Sticky barrier 粘性障碍

Sticky board system 粘板系统

Sticky museum trap 粘性博物馆陷阱，粘性博物馆诱捕器

Sticky trap 粘性诱捕器

Stigma 气孔，气门；翅痣；（卵的）眼点；点斑

Stomach poison 胃毒剂

Stop a mold bloom 阻止霉菌爆发

Stop a potential pest infestation 防止潜在的虫害

Stop an infestation 抑制虫害

Storage 存储

Storage area 存储区

Storage box 存储盒

Storage cabinet 储存柜

Storage condition 保藏方法，保藏条件

Storage container 存储装具

Storage environment condition 贮藏环境条件

Store pest 仓库虫害

Store room 储藏室

Stored in the open area 在开放空间存放

Stronger resistance 更强的抵抗力

Structural damage 结构性损坏

Structural defect 结构缺陷

Structural integrity 结构的完整性

Structural pest 建筑物内的害虫

Structural timber 结构性木材

Structural wood pest 结构性木材害虫

Sub-freezing temperature 低于冰点的温度

Sub-lethal high temperature 亚致死高温

Sublimate 升华

Subtype 子类，子类别，子类型

Suction washing 真空清洗

Sulfuryl fluoride 硫酰氟

Superficial damage 表面损伤

Supply of food 食物供应

Supply of moisture 水分供应

Supply of oxygen 供氧

Support moisture pests 滋生潮湿害虫

Surface-active agent 表面活性剂

Surfactant 表面活性剂

Surrounding area 周围地区

Surrounding environment 周围环境

Survive 存活

Surviving insect 幸存的害虫

Susceptible material 易感材料

Susceptible object 易受影响的物品

Susceptible object and artifact 易受影响的物体和人工制品

Suspected carcinogen 疑似致癌物

Sustainable pest prevention 可持续的虫害防治

Swelling 溶胀，膨胀

Symptom 症状

Synthetic adhesive 合成胶粘剂

Synthetic botanical 合成的植物药

Synthetic pyrethrin 合成除虫菊酯

T

Tapa cloth 南洋树皮纸

Tapestry 挂毯

Target pest 目标害虫

Targeted treatment 定向治理，有针对性的治理

Taxidermy 动物标本剥制术

Technical-grade insecticide 工业级杀虫剂

Temperate climate 温带气候

Temperature 温度

Temperature and humidity control 温湿度控制

Temperature and relative humidity data logger 温湿度数据记录仪

Temperature control 温控，温度控制

Temperature range 温度范围

Temperature-controlled treatment 温控处理

Tenebrio 粉虫属

Tenebrionidae 拟步甲科

Tent trap 帐篷陷阱

Termite 白蚁

Textile 纺织品

Textile care 纺织品护理

Textile or fabric pest 纺织品或织物害虫

Thaumagkossa 蟆蛸皮蠹属

Thawing process 解冻处理

The building interior 建筑物内部

The integrated pest management working group(IPM-WG) 综合虫害管理工作组

The pest fact sheet 害虫资料单

Thermal conductivity 导热系数，导热率

Thermal expansion 热膨胀；热膨胀系数；热力膨胀

Thermally robust material 耐热材料

Thorictodes 圆胸皮蠹属

Thorough vacuuming 彻底真空

Three-dimensional mycelia 三维菌丝

Threshold 限度；界限；阈值入口

Through odor 通过气味（感知，检测）

Thymol 百里香酚

Thysanura 缨尾目

Tight space 密闭的空间

Timber 木材，木料

Timber borer 木材蛀虫

Timber structure 木材结构

Tineidae 谷蛾科

Tiny insect 极小昆虫

Tissue 薄纸；棉纸

Tobacco 烟草

Tolerance 耐受

Toxic component 有毒成分

Toxic residue 有毒残留物

Toxicology 毒理学；毒物学；药物毒性

Traditional pest management 传统的有害生物管理

Trail-marking pheromone 标记信息素

Transparent oxygen barrier film 透明氧气阻隔膜

Trap catch 陷阱捕获数

Trap choice 陷阱选择

Trap type 陷阱类型

Trapping program 诱捕程序

Trapping programme 捕虫方案

Trash removal 清除垃圾

Tray-type glue-board 托盘式胶板

Treasure 珍宝

Treat infested material 处理被侵染的物品

Treatment against insect pest 害虫的防治

Treatment duration 处理的时间

Treatment for insect pest 害虫防治

Treatment method 处理方法

Treatment option 处置方案

Tribolium 拟谷盗属

Trogoderma 斑皮蠹属

Trogossitidae 谷盗科

Tunnel 虫道

Type of pest 害虫种类

Type of present pests 现存害虫的种类

U

Ultraviolet energy 紫外线能量

Ultraviolet germicidal irradiation (UVGI) cleaner 紫外线杀菌辐照清洗器

Ultraviolet light trap 紫外线陷阱，紫外线诱捕器

Underlying issue 潜在的问题

Uneven temperature 不均匀的温度

Unfavorable condition 不利条件

Unintended alteration 意外的改变

Universal standard 通用标准

Unstable dye and pigment 不稳定的染料和色素

Using traps 使用陷阱

Usual life cycle 普遍生命周期

UV (ultraviolet) 紫外线

V

Vacuum chamber 真空室

Vacuum cleaner 真空吸尘器

Vacuum cleaner brush 吸尘器刷

Vacuum fitted with a HEPA filter 装有高效微粒过滤器的真空吸尘器

Vacuum freeze dryer 真空冷冻干燥机

Vacuum fumigation 真空熏蒸

Vacuum suction pressure 真空抽吸力

Vacuum with variable suction control 可控真空处理器

Vacuuming 真空处理

Vacuuming dried mold 真空干霉菌处理

Valuable artifact 珍贵的文物

Valuable manuscript 珍贵的手稿

Vapor impermeable material 蒸汽不渗透性材料

Vapor pest strip 蒸汽杀虫条

Vapor-proof enclosure 气密外壳

Vapour-barrier container 隔汽层容器

Various genera and species 不同种属

Vegetable-based material 以植物为基础的材料

Vegetable-tanned leather 植物鞣革

Vegetative hyphae 营养菌丝

Ventilation duct 通风管道，通道

Vermin 害虫

Vertebrate pest 脊椎动物害虫

Very damp wood 非常潮湿的木材

Very fragile object 非常易碎的物品

Via 通过

Viability 可行性；生存能力；活性

Vikane (sulfuryl fluoride) 硫酰氟

Vinyl eraser 乙烯基橡皮擦

Visible damage 可见的损坏

Visual inspection 目测，肉眼检查

Void 空洞，孔洞；空隙

Volatile 挥发物；挥发性的

Volatile compound 挥发性成分；挥发性化合物；挥发性组分；挥发性物质

Vulcanized rubber sponge 硫化橡胶海绵

Vulnerable artifact 脆弱的文物；脆弱的人工制品

Vulnerable collection 易损的藏品

Vulnerable material 脆弱的材料，易受伤害的材料

Vulnerable object 易发生虫霉的对象；易受攻击的对象

W

Walk-in freezer 步入式（小型）冰库；冷藏室

Walk-in nitrogen chamber 步入式氮气室

Warehouse beetle 仓库甲虫

Warm air duct 热风管道

Warm temperature 温暖的温度

Warning system 报警系统

Washing solution 清洗溶液

Water activity 水分活性；水活度；水活性

Water-based adhesive 水基粘合剂

Water-based insecticide 水剂杀虫剂

Water bath filter vacuum cleaner 水浴过滤真空吸尘器

Water damage 水损

Water-damaged object 水损的物体

Water leaking 渗漏水

Water loss 水分流失；失水量

Water spillage or leakage 水溢出或泄露

Water vapor transmission rate (WVTR) 水蒸气透过率

Weakly resistant insect 抗性弱的昆虫

Weather stripping 挡风雨条

Webbing 网状物，蛛网

Weight loss 失重

Well fused heat-seal 熔合良好的热封

Well-maintained storage area 维护良好的存储区

Well-sealed closed storage 密封良好的封闭式储存所

Well-sealed impermeable container 密封性好且不透气的容器

Well-sealed plastic bag 密封良好的塑料袋

Wet-dry vacuum 干湿真空吸尘器

Wettable powder 可湿性粉剂

Wetting agent/surfactant 润湿剂/润湿型表面活性剂

Wheat starch paste 小麦淀粉浆糊

White ant 白蚁类

Widespread infestation 大范围虫害；大范围侵染

Winged reproductive termite 有翅繁殖蚁

Wingless insect 无翼昆虫

Wingless psocid 无翼啮虫

Wire mesh screen 网筛；金属丝筛网

Wood boring beetle 蛀木甲虫

Wood boring insect 木材钻孔昆虫

Wood-boring insect 穿孔性昆虫；蛀木昆虫

Wood cellulose 木纤维素；木材纤维素；木质纤维素

Wood-decay 木材霉腐

Wood decaying fungi 木材腐朽菌

Wood destroying organism 破坏木材的生物

Wood infesting insect/pest 木材害虫

Wood infesting insect identification chart 木材害虫鉴定图

Wood painted panel 木漆面板

Wood permeability 木材渗透性；木材透气性

Wood product 木制品

Wood shelving 木质柜架

Wood species 木材种类

Wooden art object 木制艺术品

Wooden artefact 木质人工制品

Wooden collection 木质藏品

Wooden composite 木质复合材料

Wooden object 木质物体

Wooden structure 木结构

Wool and silk based textile 丝毛织品；以羊毛和丝绸为基础的纺织品

Wool-based embroidery 羊毛刺绣

Woolen textile 毛纺织品

Work on paper 纸质作品

Worn book 旧书

Wriggling pest 蠕动的害虫

X

Xerophilic fungi 嗜干真菌

Xylothrips 长棒长蠹属

Y

Year-round storage 全年存储

Z

Zero oxygen insect treatment 零氧灭虫

Zip-lock bag 有拉链的袋子

Zygospore 接合孢子

附录一

常见馆藏害虫虫名检索

（一）中文俗名检索

A

埃及豌豆象　Egyptian pea weevil　*Bruchidius incarnatus* (Boheman)

暗褐郭公虫　clerid beetle　*Thaneroclerus buqueti* (Lefebvre)

暗褐毛皮蠹　dark brown fur beetle　*Attagenus brunneus* Faldermann

暗条豆象　dark stripes seed beetle　*Bruchidius atrolineatus* (Pic)

凹缘大蠊　Smokeybrown cockroach　*Periplaneta emarginata* Karny = *Periplaneta fuliginosa* (Serville)

澳洲大蠊　Australian cockroach　*Periplaneta australasiae* (Fabricius)

澳洲皮蠹　Australian carpet beetle　*Anthrenocerus australis* (Hope)

澳洲蛛甲　Australian spider beetle　*Ptinus tectus* Boieldieu

B

巴西豆象　Brazilian seed beetle　*Zabrotes subfasciatus* (Boheman)

白斑皮蠹　white spotted beetle　*Trogoderma megatomoides* Reitter

白斑蛛甲　white-marked spider beetle　*Ptinus fur* (Linnaeus)

白背皮蠹　white back beetle　*Dermestes dimidiatus* Steven

白带圆皮蠹　bird nest carpet beetle, panda carpet beetle　*Anthrenus pimpinellae* Fabricius

白腹皮蠹　hide beetle　*Dermestes maculatus* De Geer

白肩家蛾　white-shouldered housemoth　*Endrosis sarcitrella* (Linnaeus)

百怪皮蠹　odd beetle　*Thylodrias contractus* Motschulsky

斑胸毛皮蠹　zebra-breasted fur beetle　*Attagenus suspiciosus* Solskij

报死窃蠹，盗窃甲虫　death watch beetle　*Xestobium rufovillosum* (De Geer)

秘鲁皮蠹　Peruvian hide beetle　*Dermestes peruvianus*

扁豆象　lesser pea weevil　*Bruchus affinis* Fröelich

扁蕈甲　flat beetle　*Holoparamecus depressus* Curtis

标本圆皮蠹　museum beetle　*Anthrenus museorum* (Linnaeus)

波兰圆皮蠹　Polish round beetle　*Anthrenus polonicus* Mroczkowski

波纹长皮蠹　carpet beetle　*Megatoma undata* (Linnaeus)

波纹毛皮蠹　ripple fur beetle　*Attagenus undulatus* (Motschulsky)

波纹皮蠹　ripple beetle　*Dermestes undulatus* Brahm

博物馆甲虫（里斯皮蠹）　Museum nuisance beetle　*Reesa vespulae* (Milliron)

C

菜豆象　bean weevil, bean seed beetle　*Acanthoscelides obtectus* (Say)

仓储木阎虫　warehouse wood hister beetle　*Dendrophilus xavieri* Marseul

仓储蛛甲　warehouse spider beetle, storage spider beetle　*Tipnus unicolor* (Piller & Mitterpacher)

长斑皮蠹　Berlin beetle　*Trogoderma angustum* (Solier)

长翅露尾甲　long wings sap beetle　*Carpophilus sexpustulatus* (Fabricius)

长翅毛皮蠹　long-winged fur beetle　*Attagenus longipennis* Pic

长角扁谷盗　flat grain beetle　*Cryptolestes pusillus* (Schénherr)

长头谷盗　long-headed flour beetle　*Latheticus oryzae* Waterhouse

齿粉蠹　tooth powderpost beetle　*Lyctoxylon dentatum* (Pascoe)

赤颈郭公虫　red-shouldered ham beetle　*Necrobia ruficollis* (Fabricius)

赤毛皮蠹　red fur beetle, reddish pubescent dried fish beetle　*Dermestes tessellatocollis* Motschulsky

赤拟谷盗　red flour beetle　*Tribolium castaneum* (Herbst)

赤胸郭公虫　red-chested ham beetle　*Opetiopalpus sabulosus* Motschulsky

赤足郭公虫　red-legged ham beetle　*Necrobia rufipes* (De Geer)

厨蚁　pharaoh ant　*Monomorium pharaonis* (Linnaeus)

D

大斑螟　larger tabby　*Aglossa pinguinalis* (Linnaeus)

大谷盗　cadelle beetle　*Tenebroides mauritanicus* (Linnaeus)

大谷蠹　larger grain beetle　*Prostephanus truncatus* (Horn)

大黑粉盗　larger black flour beetle　*Cynaeus angustus* (LeConte)

大理窃蠹　wood-boring beetle　*Ptilineurus marmoratus* (Reitter)

大眼锯谷盗　merchant grain beetle　*Oryzaephilus mercator* (Fauvel)

大眼薪甲　big eyes beetle, bigeye beetle　*Dienerella arga* (Reitter)

大腋露尾甲　brownish sap beetle　*Carpophilus marginellus* Motschulsky

淡带皮蠹　light belt beetle　*Dermestes vorax var. albofasciatus* Matsumura & Yokoyama

档案窃蠹　archives beetle　*Falsogastrallus sauteri* Pic

德国小蠊　German cockroach　*Blattella germanica* (Linnaeus)

地毯圆皮蠹　common carpet beetle, buffalo carpet beetle　*Anthrenus scrophulariae* (Linnaeus)

地中海螟　Mediterranean flour moth　*Ephestia kuehniella* Zeller

东方蜚蠊，东方小蠊　oriental cockroach　*Blatta orientalis* Linnaeus

东方薪甲　oriental beetle　*Migneauxia orientalis* Reitter

东非毛皮蠹　East African fur beetle　*Attagenus insidiosus* Halstead

东南亚锯谷盗　Southeast Asia saw-toothed grain beetle　*Silvanoprus cephalotes* (Reitter)

短角褐毛皮蠹　black carpet beetle　*Attagenus unicolor simulans* Solskij

短角露尾甲　short angle sap beetle　*Omosita colon* (Linnaeus)

短毛蛛甲　short hair spider beetle　*Ptinus sexpunctatus* Panzer

多斑圆皮蠹　spotty round beetle　*Anthrenus maculifer* Reitter

E

二带黑菌虫　two-banded fungus beetle　*Alphitophagus bifasciatus* (Say)

二点地毯甲虫，二星毛皮蠹　fur beetle, carpet beetle　*Attagenus pellio* (Linnaeus)

二色球棒甲　two-color bat beetle, two colors ball stick armour　*Monotoma bicolor* Villa & Villa

二纹露尾甲　two-spotted sap beetle　*Nitidula bipunctata* (Linnaeus)

F

方胸粉蠹　powderpost beetle　*Trogoxylon impressum* (Comolli)

非洲粉蠹　Africa powderpost beetle　*Lyctus africanus* Lesne

非洲褐菌虫　Africa brown fungus beetle, brown fungus beetle of Africa　*Alphitobius viator* Mulsant & Godart

粉斑螟　almond moth　*Ephestia cautella* (Walker)

粉蠹虫，菌蠹虫　Ambrosia beetle

伏特加甲虫　Vodka beetle　*Attagenus smirnovi* Zhantiev

G

甘薯小象甲　sweet potato weevil　*Cylas formicarius* (Fabricius)

高加索圆皮蠹　Caucasus round beetle　*Anthrenus caucasicus* Reitter

根西皮蠹，格恩西岛地毯甲虫　Guernsey carpet beetle　*Anthrenus sarnicus* Mroczkowski

钩角隐食甲　acute angled fungus beetle　*Cryptophagus acutangulus* Gyllenhal

钩纹皮蠹　black larder beetle, incinerator beetle　*Dermestes ater* De Geer

谷斑皮蠹　Khapra beetle　*Trogoderma granarium* Everts

谷蠹　lesser grain borer　*Rhyzopertha dominica* (Fabricius)

谷拟叩甲　Mexican grain beetle　*Pharaxonotha kirschii* Reitter

谷象　granary seed beetle　*Sitophilus granarius* (Linnaeus)

谷蚁形甲　ant-like beetle, narrownecked grain beetle　*Anthicus floralis* (Linnaeus)

谷蛛甲　shiny spider beetle, northern spider beetle, hood spider beetle　*Mezium affine* Boieldieu

广大腿小蜂，黄大腿蜂　chalcid wasp　*Brachymeria obscurata* (Walker)

H

褐斑大蠊　brown cockroach, Southern brown cockroach　*Periplaneta brunnea* Burmeister

褐带皮蠊　brownbanded cockroach　*Supella longipalpa* (Fabricius)

褐簟甲　pleasing fungus beetle　*Cryptophilus integer* (Heer）

褐粉蠹，竹褐粉蠹　brown powderpost beetle　*Lyctus brunneus* (Stephens)

褐家蛾，褐织蛾，拟衣蛾　brown house moth　*Hofmannophila pseudospretella* (Stainton)

褐毛皮蠹　brown fur beetle　*Attagenus augustatus gobicola* Frivaldszky

褐拟谷盗　false black flour beetle　*Tribolium destructor* Uyttenboogaart

褐蛛甲　brown spider beetle　*Pseudeurostus hilleri* (Reitter)

黑矮甲阎虫　poultryhouse pill beetle　*Carcinops pumilio* (Erichson)

黑斑豆象　dark spots seed beetle, black spotted weevil　*Bruchus dentipes* Baudi

黑斑皮蠹　glabrous cabinet beetle, colored cabinet beetle　*Trogoderma glabrum* (Herbst)

黑粉虫　dark mealworm　*Tenebrio obscurus* Fabricius

黑菌虫　lesser mealworm　*Alphitobius diaperinus* Panzer

黑毛皮蠹，黑皮蠹　black carpet beetle　*Attagenus unicolor japonicus* Reitter

黑拟谷盗　black flour beetle　*Tribolium madens* (Charpentier)

黑尾拟天牛　wharf borer　*Nacerdes melanura* (Linnaeus)

黑圆皮蠹　carpet beetle　*Anthrenus fuscus* Olivier

红带皮蠹　red belt beetle　*Dermestes vorax* Motschulsky

红角拟步甲　red-horned darkling beetle　*Platydema ruficorne* (Stürm)

红颈薪甲　minute brown scavenger beetle　*Dienerella ruficollis* (Marsham)

花斑皮蠹　warehouse beetle　*Trogoderma variabile* Ballion

黄带圆皮蠹　Asian carpet beetle　*Anthrenus coloratus* Reitter

黄粉虫　yellow mealworm beetle　*Tenebrio molitor* Linnaeus

黄胸木蜂　Japanese carpenter bee　*Xylocopa appendiculata* Smith

黄蛛甲，黄金蛛甲　golden spider beetle　*Niptus hololeucus* (Faldermann)

灰豆象　dolichos seed beetle　*Callosobruchus phaseoli* (Gyllenhal)

灰泥甲虫　plaster beetle　*Cartodere constricta* (Gryllenhal)

灰衣鱼，蠹鱼，衣鱼　silverfish　*Ctenolepisma longicaudata* Escherich

火腿皮蠹　larder beetle　*Dermestes lardarius* Linnaeus

J

姬粉盗　small-eyed flour beetle　*Palorus ratzeburgi* (Wissmann)

脊胸露尾甲　corn sap beetle　*Carpophilus dimidiatus* (Fabricius)

家褐蚁　longhorn crazy ant　*Paratrechina longicornis* (Lattreille)

家具窃蠹　furniture beetle　*Anobium punctatum* (De Geer)

家蠊，家屋斑蠊　harlequin cockroach　*Neostylopyga rhombifolia* (Stoll)

家茸天牛　velvet long horned beetle　*Trichoferus campestris* (Faldermann)

家天牛　house longhorn beetle　*Stromatium longicorne* (Newman)

家庭钩纹皮蠹　domestic black larder beetle　*Dermestes ater domesticus* Germar

家蟋蟀　house cricket　*Acheta domesticus* (Linnaeus)

家希天牛　European house borer　*Hylotrupes bajulus* (Linnaeus)

家衣鱼　firebrat　*Thermobia domestica* (Packard)

加州粉蠹　California powderpost beetle　*Trogoxylon aequale* (Wollaston)

箭斑圆皮蠹　arrow spot round beetle　*Anthrenus picturatus* Solskij

酱曲露尾甲，黄斑露尾甲　driedfruit beetle　*Carpophilus hemipterus* (Linnaeus)

角扁谷盗　horn grain beetle　*Cryptolestes cornutus* Thomas & Zimmerman

金黄圆皮蠹　golden round beetle　*Anthrenus flavidus* Solskij

锯谷盗　saw-toothed grain beetle　*Oryzaephilus surinamensis* (Linnaeus)

K

咖啡长角象（咖啡豆象）　coffee bean weevil　*Araecerus fasciculatus* (De Geer)

咖啡果小蠹　coffee berry borer　*Hypothenemus hampei* (Ferrari)

可可豆象　cocoa seed beetle　*Callosobruchus theobromae* (Linnaeus)

阔鼻谷象　broad-nosed grain weevil　*Caulophilus oryzae* (Gyllenhal)

阔角谷盗　broad-horned flour beetle　*Gnathocerus cornutus* (Fabricius)

L

丽黄圆皮蠹　furniture carpet beetle　*Anthrenus flavipes* LeConte

栎粉蠹　European lyctus beetle　*Lyctus linearis* (Goeze)

鳞毛粉蠹　powderpost beetle, hairy powder-post beetle　*Minthea rugicollis* (Walker)

六点蛛甲　six spots spider beetle　*Ptinus exulans* Erichson

隆肩露尾甲　souring beetle　*Urophorus humeralis* (Fabricius)

罗得西亚豆象　Rhodesian bean seed beetle　*Callosobruchus rhodesianus* (Pic)

罗望子象　tamarind seed beetle　*Sitophilus linearis* (Herbst)

绿豆象　southern cowpea weevil, azuki seed beetle　*Callosobruchus chinensis* (Linnaeus)

M

麻头堆砂白蚁　West Indian drywood termite　*Cryptotermes brevis* (Walker)

麦蛾　Angoumois grain moth　*Sitotroga cerealella* (Olivier)

玫瑰皮蠹　rose beetle　*Dermestes dimidiatus ab.rosea* Kusnezova

美西粉蠹　western lyctus beetle　*Lyctus cavicollis* LeConte

美洲大蠊　American cockroach　*Periplaneta americana* (Linnaeus)

美洲黑拟谷盗　American black flour beetle　*Tribolium audax* Halstead

美洲皮蠹　Americana beetle　*Dermestes nidum* Arrow

米扁虫　foreign grain beetle　*Ahasverus advena* (Waltl)

米淡墨虫，米织蛾　grain worm　*Anchonoma xeraula* Meyrick

米黑虫　black rice worm　*Aglossa dimidiata* (Haworth)

米象　rice weevil　*Sitophilus oryzae* (Linnaeus)

棉露尾甲　yellow-brown sap beetle　*Haptoncus luteolus* (Erichson)

缅甸毛皮蠹　Burmese fur beetle　*Attagenus birmanicus* Arrow

墨西哥斑皮蠹　Mexican spotted beetle　*Trogoderma anthrenoides* (Sharp)

木蠹虫，家具甲虫　woodworm　*Anobium punctatum* (De Geer)

木蚁，黑木蚁　black carpenter ant　*Camponotus pennsylvanicus* (De Geer)

幕谷蛾，幕衣蛾　common clothes moth　*Tineola bisselliella* (Hummel)

N

拟白腹皮蠹　fringed larder beetle　*Dermestes frischii* Kugelann

拟裸蛛甲　smooth spider beetle　*Gibbium aequinoctiale* Boieldieu

拟肾斑皮蠹　European larger cabinet beetle　*Trogoderma versicolor* (Creutzer)

柠条豆象　caragana seed beetle　*Kytorhinus immixtus* Motschulsky

浓毛窃蠹　pubescent anobiid　*Nicobium castaneum* (Olivier)

O

欧洲砂潜　darkling beetle　*Opatrum sabulosum* (Linnaeus)

P

皮氏书虱　book louse　*Liposcelis pearmani* Lienhard

Q

青蓝郭公虫　black-legged ham beetle　*Necrobia violacea* (Linnaeus)

球蛛甲　globular spider beetle　*Trigonogenius globulum* (Solier)

R

热带烟草螟　tropical tobacco moth　*Setomorpha rutella* Zeller

日本斑皮蠹　japonicus spotted beetle　*Trogoderma varium* (Matsumura & Yokoyama)

日本大蠊　Japanese cockroach　*Periplaneta japonica* Karny

日本球棒皮蠹　Japanese bat beetle　*Orphinus japonicas* Arrow

日本蛛甲　spider beetle　*Ptinus japonicus* Reitter

柔毛长皮蠹　pilose long beetle　*Megatoma pubescens* (Zetterstedt)

肉食皮蠹　hide beetle　*Dermestes carnivorus* Fabricius

S

三带毛皮蠹　three-banded fur beetle　*Attagenus sinensis* Pic

三叶草豆象　clover seed beetle　*Bruchidius trifolii* (Motschulsky)

肾斑皮蠹　larger cabinet beetle　*Trogoderma inclusum* LeConte

湿薪甲　squarenosed fungus beetle　*Lathridius minutus* (Linnaeus)

饰斑皮蠹　ornat cabinet beetle　*Trogoderma ornatum* (Say)

嗜卷书虱　booklouse　*Liposcelis bostrychophila* Badonnel

梳角细脉窃蠹　Fan-bearing wood-borer　*Ptilinus pectinicornis* (Linnaeus)

双齿长蠹　stored derris root bostrychid　*Sinoxylon anale* Lesne

双齿锯谷盗　flat bark beetle　*Silvanus bidentatus* (Fabricius)

双带皮蠹　double belt beetle　*Dermestes coarctatus* Harold

双窝竹长蠹　auger beetle　*Dinoderus bifoveolatus* (Wollaston)

斯氏毛皮蠹，棕色地毯甲虫　brown carpet beetle　*Attagenus smirnovi* Zhantiev

四斑蕈甲，四纹蕈甲　spotted hairy fungus beetle　*Mycetophagus quadriguttatus* Müller

四行薪甲　ridge winged fungus beetle　*Lathredius bergrothi* (Reitter)

四纹长皮蠹　four-streaked long beetle　*Megatoma graeseri* (Reitter)

四纹豆象　cowpea seed beetle, cowpea weevil　*Callosobruchus maculatus* (Fabricius)

四纹蛛甲　hairy spider beetle　*Ptinus villiger* (Reitter)

T

台湾乳白蚁，家白蚁　oriental termite　*Coptotermes formosanus* Shiraki

条斑皮蠹　streak beetle　*Trogoderma teukton* Beal

头角扁薪甲　head horn flat beetle　*Holoparamecus signatus* Wollaston

凸蛛甲　spider beetle　*Sphaericus gibboides* (Boieldieu)

土耳其扁谷盗　flourmill beetle, Turkish grain beetle　*Cryptolestes turcicus* (Grouvelle)

椭圆扁薪甲　elliptica flat beetle　*Holoparamecus ellipticus* Wollaston

W

豌豆象　pea weevil, pea beetle　*Bruchus pisorum* (Linnaeus)

无色书虱　book louse　*Liposcelis decolor* (Pearman) = *Liposcelis simulans* Broadhead

X

西北蛛甲　north-west spider beetle　*Mezioniptus impressicollis* Pic

西伯利亚皮蠹　Siberia beetle　*Dermestes sibiricus* Erichson

西部干木白蚁，干木切白蚁　Western drywood termite　*Incisitermes minor* (Hagen)

西非豆象　West Africa seed beetle　*Callosobruchus subinnotatus* (Pic)

细角谷盗　slender-horned flour beetle　*Gnathocerus maxillosus* (Fabricius)

暹罗谷盗　bark-gnawing beetle　*Lophocateres pusillus* (Klug)

小斑螟　lesser tabby　*Aglossa caprealis* (Hübner)

小粉盗　small flour beetle　*Palorus cerylonoides* (Pascoe)

小菌虫　black fungus beetle　*Alphitobius laevigatus* (Panzer)

小露尾甲　small sap beetle　*Carpophllus pilosellus* Motschulsky

小圆虫　murmidius beetle　*Murmidius ovalis* (Beck)

小圆皮蠹，多变的地毯甲虫　varied carpet beetle　*Anthrenus verbasci* (Linnaeus)

小圆胸皮蠹　carpet beetle　*Thorictodes heydeni* Reitter

小竹长蠹　auger beetle　*Dinoderus brevis* Horn

斜带褐毛皮蠹　inclined belt brown fur beetle　*Attagenus augustatus* Ballion

胸斑皮蠹　carpet beetle　*Trogoderma sternale* Jayne

锈赤扁谷盗　flat grain beetle, red-rust grain beetle　*Cryptolestes ferrugineus* (Stephens)

Y

亚扁粉盗　depressed flour beetle　*Palorus subdepressus* (Wollaston)

亚非扁谷盗　flat grain beetle　*Cryptolestes klapperichi* Lefkovitch

亚洲天牛　Asian long-horned beetle　*Anoplophora glabripennis* (Motschulsky)

烟草甲，香烟甲虫，烟草窃蠹　cigarette beetle, cigar beetle, tobacco beetle　*Lasioderma serricorne* (Fabricius)

烟草螟　tobacco moth　*Ephestia elutella* (Hübner)

洋虫　drug darkling beetle　*Martianus dermestoides* (Chevrolat)

药材甲，药材甲虫，饼干甲虫　drugstore beetle, biscuit beetle, bread beetle　*Stegobium paniceum* (Linnaeus)

野葛豆象　kudzu seed beetle　*Callosobruchus ademptus* (Sharp)

野豌豆象　vetch bruchid　*Bruchus brachialis* Fåhraeus

一点谷蛾　stored nut moth　*Aphomia gularis* (Zeller)

银合欢豆象　leucaena beetle　*Acanthoscelides macrophthalmus* (Schaeffer)

印度大甲虫　Atlas beetle　*Chalcosoma atlas* (Linnaeus)

印度谷螟，印度谷斑螟　Indian meal moth　*Plodia interpunctella*

(Hübner)

印度皮蠹　Indian beetle　*Dermestes leechi* Kalik

鹰嘴豆象　graham bean weevil　*Callosobruchus analis* (Fabricius)

玉米象　maize seed weevil　*Sitophilus zeamais* Motschulsky

云南斑皮蠹　Yunnan spotted beetle　*Trogoderma yunnaeunsis* Zhang & Liu

Z

杂木蛀虫　miscellaneous wood borer

杂拟谷盗　confused flour beetle　*Tribolium confusum* Jacquelin du Val

皂荚豆象　gleditsia sinensis seed beetle　*Bruchidius dorsalis* (Fåhraeus)

蔗蠊　Surinam cockroach　*Pycnoscelus surinamensis* (Linnaeus)

中华粉蠹　Chinese powderpost beetle　*Lyctus sinensis* Lesne

中华圆皮蠹　Chinese round beetle　*Anthrenus sinensis* Arrow

中亚皮蠹　Central Asia beetle　*Dermestes elegans* Gebler

竹长蠹　bamboo borer　*Dinoderus minutus* (Fabricius)

竹虎天牛　bamboo longhorn beetle　*Chlorophorus annularis* (Fabricius)

紫斑谷螟　meal moth　*Pyralis farinalis* (Linnaeus)

棕长毛皮蠹　long brown hair beetle　*Trinodes rufescens* Reitter

棕榈核小蠹　date stone beetle　*Coccotrypes dactyliperda* (Fabricius)

棕蛛甲　brown spider beetle　*Ptinus clavipes* Panzer

（二）英文俗名检索

A

acute angled fungus beetle　*Cryptophagus acutangulus* Gyllenhal　钩角隐食甲

Africa brown fungus beetle　*Alphitobius viator* Mulsant & Godart　非洲褐菌虫

Africa powderpost beetle　*Lyctus africanus* Lesne　非洲粉蠹

almond moth　*Ephestia cautella* (Walker)　粉斑螟

Ambrosia beetle　粉蠹虫，菌蠹虫

American black flour beetle　*Tribolium audax* Halstead　美洲黑拟谷盗

American cockroach　*Periplaneta americana* (Linnaeus)　美洲大蠊

Americana beetle　*Dermestes nidum* Arrow　美洲皮蠹

Angoumois grain moth　*Sitotroga cerealella* (Olivier)　麦蛾

ant-like beetle　*Anthicus floralis* (Linnaeus)　谷蚁形甲

archives beetle　*Falsogastrallus sauteri* Pic　档案窃蠹

arrow spot round beetle　*Anthrenus picturatus* Solskij　箭斑圆皮蠹

Asian carpet beetle *Anthrenus coloratus* Reitter 黄带圆皮蠹

Asian long-horned beetle *Anoplophora glabripennis* (Motschulsky) 亚洲天牛

Atlas beetle *Chalcosoma atlas* (Linnaeus) 印度大甲虫

auger beetle *Dinoderus bifoveolatus* (Wollaston) 双窝竹长蠹；
　　　　　Dinoderus brevis Horn 小竹长蠹

Australian carpet beetle *Anthrenocerus australis* (Hope) 澳洲皮蠹

Australian cockroach *Periplaneta australasiae* (Fabricius) 澳洲大蠊

Australian spider beetle *Ptinus tectus* Boieldieu 澳洲蛛甲

azuki seed beetle *Callosobruchus chinensis* (Linnaeus) 绿豆象

B

bamboo borer *Dinoderus minutus* (Fabricius) 竹长蠹

bamboo borer, bamboo longhorn beetle *Chlorophorus annularis* (Fabricius) 竹虎天牛

bark-gnawing beetle *Lophocateres pusillus* (Klug) 暹罗谷盗

bean weevil, bean seed beetle *Acanthoscelides obtectus* (Say) 菜豆象

Berlin beetle *Trogoderma angustum* (Solier) 长斑皮蠹

bigeye beetle, big eyes beetle *Dienerella arga* (Reitter) 大眼薪甲

bird nest carpet beetle *Anthrenus pimpinellae* Fabricius 白带圆皮蠹

biscuit beetle *Stegobium paniceum* (Linnaeus) 药材甲，药材甲虫，饼干甲虫

black carpenter ant *Camponotus pennsylvanicus* (De Geer) 木蚁，黑木蚁

black carpet beetle *Attagenus unicolor simulans* Solskij 短角褐毛皮蠹；

Attagenus unicolor japonicus Reitter 黑毛皮蠹，黑皮蠹

black flour beetle *Tribolium madens* (Charpentier) 黑拟谷盗

black fungus beetle *Alphitobius laevigatus* (Panzer) 小菌虫

black larder beetle *Dermestes ater* De Geer 钩纹皮蠹

black-legged ham beetle *Necrobia violacea* (Linnaeus) 青蓝郭公虫

black rice worm *Aglossa dimidiata* (Haworth) 米黑虫

black spotted weevil *Bruchus dentipes* Baudi 黑斑豆象

book louse *Liposcelis decolor* (Pearman)=*Liposcelis simulans* Broadhead 无色书虱；

Liposcelis pearmani Lienhard 皮氏书虱

booklouse *Liposcelis bostrychophila* Badonnel 嗜卷书虱

Brazilian seed beetle *Zabrotes subfasciatus* (Boheman) 巴西豆象

bread beetle *Stegobium paniceum* (Linnaeus) 药材甲，药材甲虫，饼干甲虫

broad-horned flour beetle   *Gnathocerus cornutus* (Fabricius)   阔角谷盗

broad-nosed grain weevil   *Caulophilus oryzae* (Gyllenhal)   阔鼻谷象

brown carpet beetle   *Attagenus smirnovi* Zhantiev   斯氏毛皮蠹，棕色地毯甲虫

brown cockroach, Southern brown cockroach   *Periplaneta brunnea* Burmeister   褐斑大蠊

brown fungus beetle of Africa   *Alphitobius viator* Mulsant & Godart   非洲褐菌虫

brown fur beetle   *Attagenus augustatus gobicola* Frivaldszky   褐毛皮蠹

brown house moth   *Hofmannophila pseudospretella* (Stainton)   褐家蛾，褐织蛾，拟衣蛾

brown powderpost beetle   *Lyctus brunneus* (Stephens)   褐粉蠹，竹褐粉蠹

brown spider beetle   *Pseudeurostus hilleri* (Reitter)   褐蛛甲；
　　　　　　　　　　Ptinus clavipes Panzer   棕蛛甲

brownbanded cockroach   *Supella longipalpa* (Fabricius)   褐带皮蠊

brownish sap beetle   *Carpophilus marginellus* Motschulsky   大腋露尾甲

buffalo carpet beetle   *Anthrenus scrophulariae* (Linnaeus)   地毯圆皮蠹

Burmese fur beetle   *Attagenus birmanicus* Arrow   缅甸毛皮蠹

C

cadelle beetle　*Tenebroides mauritanicus* (Linnaeus)　大谷盗

California powderpost beetle　*Trogoxylon aequale* (Wollaston)　加州粉蠹

caragana seed beetle　*Kytorhinus immixtus* Motschulsky　柠条豆象

carpet beetle　*Thorictodes heydeni* Reitter　小圆胸皮蠹；

　　　　　Anthrenus fuscus Olivier　黑圆皮蠹；

　　　　　Attagenus pellio (Linnaeus)　二点地毯甲虫，二星毛皮蠹；

　　　　　Megatoma undata (Linnaeus)　波纹长皮蠹；

　　　　　Trogoderma sternale Jayne　胸斑皮蠹

Caucasus round beetle　*Anthrenus caucasicus* Reitter　高加索圆皮蠹

Central Asia beetle　*Dermestes elegans* Gebler　中亚皮蠹

chalcid wasp　*Brachymeria obscurata* (Walker)　广大腿小蜂，黄大腿蜂

Chinese powderpost beetle　*Lyctus sinensis* Lesne　中华粉蠹

Chinese round beetle　*Anthrenus sinensis* Arrow　中华圆皮蠹

cigar beetle, cigarette beetle　*Lasioderma serricorne* (Fabricius)　烟草甲，香烟甲虫，烟草窃蠹

clerid beetle　*Thaneroclerus buqueti* (Lefebvre)　暗褐郭公虫

clover seed beetle　*Bruchidius trifolii* (Motschulsky)　三叶草豆象

cocoa seed beetle　*Callosobruchus theobromae* (Linnaeus)　可可豆象

coffee bean weevil　*Araecerus fasciculatus* (De Geer)　咖啡长角象（咖啡豆象）

coffee berry borer　*Hypothenemus hampei* (Ferrari)　咖啡果小蠹

colored cabinet beetle　*Trogoderma glabrum* (Herbst)　黑斑皮蠹

common carpet beetle　*Anthrenus scrophulariae* (Linnaeus)　地毯圆皮蠹

common clothes moth　*Tineola bisselliella* (Hummel)　幕谷蛾，幕衣蛾

confused flour beetle　*Tribolium confusum* Jacquelin du Val　杂拟谷盗

corn sap beetle　*Carpophilus dimidiatus* (Fabricius)　脊胸露尾甲

cowpea seed beetle, cowpea weevil　*Callosobruchus maculatus* (Fabricius)　四纹豆象

D

dark brown fur beetle　*Attagenus brunneus* Faldermann　暗褐毛皮蠹

dark mealworm　*Tenebrio obscurus* Fabricius　黑粉虫

dark spots seed beetle　*Bruchus dentipes* Baudi　黑斑豆象

dark stripes seed beetle　*Bruchidius atrolineatus* (Pic)　暗条豆象

darkling beetle　*Opatrum sabulosum* (Linnaeus)　欧洲砂潜

date stone beetle　*Coccotrypes dactyliperda* (Fabricius)　棕榈核小蠹

death watch beetle　*Xestobium rufovillosum* (De Geer)　报死窃蠹，盗窃甲虫

depressed flour beetle　　*Palorus subdepressus* (Wollaston)　　亚扁粉盗

dolichos seed beetle　　*Callosobruchus phaseoli* (Gyllenhal)　　灰豆象

domestic black larder beetle　　*Dermestes ater domesticus* Germar　　家庭钩纹皮蠹

double belt beetle　　*Dermestes coarctatus* Harold　　双带皮蠹

driedfruit beetle　　*Carpophilus hemipterus* (Linnaeus)　　酱曲露尾甲，黄斑露尾甲

drug darkling beetle　　*Martianus dermestoides* (Chevrolat)　　洋虫

drugstore beetle　　*Stegobium paniceum* (Linnaeus)　　药材甲，药材甲虫，饼干甲虫

E

East African fur beetle　　*Attagenus insidiosus* Halstead　　东非毛皮蠹

Egyptian pea weevil　　*Bruchidius incarnatus* (Boheman)　　埃及豌豆象

elliptica flat beetle　　*Holoparamecus ellipticus* Wollaston　　椭圆扁薪甲

European house borer　　*Hylotrupes bajulus* (Linnaeus)　　家希天牛

European larger cabinet beetle　　*Trogoderma versicolor* (Creutzer)　　拟肾斑皮蠹

European lyctus beetle　　*Lyctus linearis* (Goeze)　　栎粉蠹

F

false black flour beetle　*Tribolium destructor* Uyttenboogaart　褐拟谷盗

fan-bearing wood-borer　*Ptilinus pectinicornis* (Linnaeus)　梳角细脉窃蠹

firebrat　*Thermobia domestica* (Packard)　家衣鱼

flat bark beetle　*Silvanus bidentatus* (Fabricius)　双齿锯谷盗

flat beetle　*Holoparamecus depressus* Curtis　扁薪甲

flat grain beetle　*Cryptolestes pusillus* (Schénherr)　长角扁谷盗；

　　　　　　　　Cryptolestes ferrugineus (Stephens)　锈赤扁谷盗；

　　　　　　　　Cryptolestes klapperichi Lefkovitch　亚非扁谷盗

flourmill beetle　*Cryptolestes turcicus* (Grouvelle)　土耳其扁谷盗

foregin grain beetle　*Ahasverus advena* (Waltl)　米扁虫

four-streaked long beetle　*Megatoma graeseri* (Reitter)　四纹长皮蠹

fringed larder beetle　*Dermestes frischii* Kugelann　拟白腹皮蠹

fur beetle　*Attagenus pellio* (Linnaeus)　二点地毯甲虫，二星毛皮蠹

furniture beetle　*Anobium punctatum* (De Geer)　家具窃蠹

furniture carpet beetle　*Anthrenus flavipes* LeConte　丽黄圆皮蠹

G

German cockroach　*Blattella germanica* (Linnaeus)　德国小蠊

glabrous cabinet beetle　　*Trogoderma glabrum* (Herbst)　　黑斑皮蠹

gleditsia sinensis seed beetle　　*Bruchidius dorsalis* (Fåhraeus)　　皂荚豆象

globular spider beetle　　*Trigonogenius globulum* (Solier)　　球蛛甲

golden round beetle　　*Anthrenus flavidus* Solskij　　金黄圆皮蠹

golden spider beetle　　*Niptus hololeucus* (Faldermann)　　黄蛛甲，黄金蛛甲

graham bean weevil　　*Callosobruchus analis* (Fabricius)　　鹰嘴豆象

grain worm　　*Anchonoma xeraula* Meyrick　　米淡墨虫，米织蛾

granary seed beetle　　*Sitophilus granarius* (Linnaeus)　　谷象

Guernsey carpet beetle　　*Anthrenus sarnicus* Mroczkowski　　根西皮蠹，格恩西岛地毯甲虫

H

hairy spider beetle　　*Ptinus villiger* (Reitter)　　四纹蛛甲

harlequin cockroach　　*Neostylopyga rhombifolia* (Stoll)　　家蠊，家屋斑蠊

head horn flat beetle　　*Holoparamecus signatus* Wollaston　　头角扁薪甲

hide beetle　　*Dermestes maculatus* De Geer　　白腹皮蠹；

　　　　　　　Dermestes carnivorus Fabricius　　肉食皮蠹

hood spider beetle　　*Mezium affine* Boieldieu　　谷蛛甲

horn grain beetle　　*Cryptolestes cornutus* Thomas & Zimmerman　　角扁谷盗

house cricket　　*Acheta domesticus* (Linnaeus)　　家蟋蟀

house longhorn beetle　*Stromatium longicorne* (Newman)　家天牛

I

incinerator beetle　*Dermestes ater* De Geer　钩纹皮蠹

inclined belt brown fur beetle　*Attagenus augustatus* Ballion　斜带褐毛皮蠹

Indian beetle　*Dermestes leechi* Kalik　印度皮蠹

Indian meal moth　*Plodia interpunctella* (Hübner)　印度谷螟，印度谷斑螟

J

Japanese bat beetle　*Orphinus japonicus* Arrow　日本球棒皮蠹

Japanese carpenter bee　*Xylocopa appendiculata* Smith　黄胸木蜂

Japanese cockroach　*Periplaneta japonica* Karny　日本大蠊

japonicus spotted beetle　*Trogoderma varium* (Matsumura & Yokoyama)　日本斑皮蠹

K

Khapra beetle　*Trogoderma granarium* Everts　谷斑皮蠹

kudzu seed beetle　*Callosobruchus ademptus* (Sharp)　野葛豆象

L

larder beetle   *Dermestes lardarius* Linnaeus   火腿皮蠹

larger black flour beetle   *Cynaeus angustus* (LeConte)   大黑粉盗

larger cabinet beetle   *Trogoderma inclusum* LeConte   肾斑皮蠹

larger grain beetle   *Prostephanus truncatus* (Horn)   大谷蠹

larger tabby   *Aglossa pinguinalis* (Linnaeus)   大斑螟

lesser grain borer   *Rhyzopertha dominica* (Fabricius)   谷蠹

lesser mealworm   *Alphitobius diaperinus* Panzer   黑菌虫

lesser pea weevil   *Bruchus affinis* Fröelich   扁豆象

lesser tabby   *Aglossa caprealis* (Hübner)   小斑螟

leucaena beetle   *Acanthoscelides macrophthalmus* (Schaeffer)   银合欢豆象

light belt beetle   *Dermestes vorax var.albofasciatus* Matsumura & Yokoyama   淡带皮蠹

long brown hair beetle   *Trinodes rufescens* Reitter   棕长毛皮蠹

long-headed flour beetle   *Latheticus oryzae* Waterhouse   长头谷盗

long-winged fur beetle   *Attagenus longipennis* Pic   长翅毛皮蠹

long wings sap beetle   *Carpophilus sexpustulatus* (Fabricius)   长翅露尾甲

longhorn crazy ant   *Paratrechina longicornis* (Lattreille)   家褐蚁

M

maize seed weevil　*Sitophilus zeamais* Motschulsky　玉米象

meal moth　*Pyralis farinalis* (Linnaeus)　紫斑谷螟

Mediterranean flour moth　*Ephestia kuehniella* Zeller　地中海螟

merchant grain beetle　*Oryzaephilus mercator* (Fauvel)　大眼锯谷盗

Mexican grain beetle　*Pharaxonotha kirschii* Reitter　谷拟叩甲

Mexican spotted beetle　*Trogoderma anthrenoides* (Sharp)　墨西哥斑皮蠹

minute brown scavenger beetle　*Dienerella ruficollis* (Marsham)　红颈薪甲

miscellaneous wood borer　杂木蛀虫

murmidius beetle　*Murmidius ovalis* (Beck)　小圆虫

museum beetle　*Anthrenus museorum* (Linnaeus)　标本圆皮蠹

museum nuisance beetle　*Reesa vespulae* (Milliron)　博物馆甲虫（里斯皮蠹）

N

north-west spider beetle　*Mezioniptus impressicollis* Pic　西北蛛甲

northern spider beetle　*Mezium affine* Boieldieu　谷蛛甲

O

odd beetle　*Thylodrias contractus* Motschulsky　百怪皮蠹

oriental beetle　*Migneauxia orientalis* Reitter　东方薪甲

oriental cockroach　*Blatta orientalis* Linnaeus　东方蜚蠊；东方小蠊

oriental termite　*Coptotermes formosanus* Shiraki　台湾乳白蚁，家白蚁

ornat cabinet beetle　*Trogoderma ornatum* (Say)　饰斑皮蠹

P

panda carpet beetle　*Anthrenus pimpinellae* Fabricius　白带圆皮蠹

pea beetle, pea weevil　*Bruchus pisorum* (Linnaeus)　豌豆象

Peruvian hide beetle　*Dermestes peruvianus*　秘鲁皮蠹

pharaoh ant　*Monomorium pharaonis* (Linnaeus)　厨蚁

pilose long beetle　*Megatoma pubescens* (Zetterstedt)　柔毛长皮蠹

plaster beetle　*Cartodere constricta* (Gryllenhal)　灰泥甲虫

pleasing fungus beetle　*Cryptophilus integer* (Heer)　褐簟甲

Polish round beetle　*Anthrenus polonicus* Mroczkowski　波兰圆皮蠹

poultryhouse pill beetle　*Carcinops pumilio* (Erichson)　黑矮甲阎虫

powderpost beetle　*Trogoxylon impressum* (Comolli)　方胸粉蠹

powderpost beetle, hairy powder-post beetle　*Minthea rugicollis* (Walker)

鳞毛粉蠹

pubescent anobiid　*Nicobium castaneum* (Olivier)　浓毛窃蠹

R

red belt beetle　*Dermestes vorax* Motschulsky　红带皮蠹

red-chested ham beetle　*Opetiopalpus sabulosus* Motschulsky　赤胸郭公虫

red flour beetle　*Tribolium castaneum* (Herbst)　赤拟谷盗

red fur beetle　*Dermestes tessellatocollis* Motschulsky　赤毛皮蠹

red-horned darkling beetle　*Platydema ruficorne* (Stürm)　红角拟步甲

red-legged ham beetle　*Necrobia rufipes* (De Geer)　赤足郭公虫

red-rust grain beetle　*Cryptolestes ferrugineus* (Stephens)　锈赤扁谷盗

red-shouldered ham beetle　*Necrobia ruficollis* (Fabricius)　赤颈郭公虫

reddish pubescent dried fish beetle　*Dermestes tessellatocollis* Motschulsky　赤毛皮蠹，赤毛鲞蠹

Rhodesian bean seed beetle　*Callosobruchus rhodesianus* (Pic)　罗得西亚豆象

rice weevil　*Sitophilus oryzae* (Linnaeus)　米象

ridge winged fungus beetle　*Lathredius bergrothi* (Reitter)　四行薪甲

ripple beetle　*Dermestes undulatus* Brahm　波纹皮蠹

ripple fur beetle　*Attagenus undulatus* (Motschulsky)　波纹毛皮蠹

rose beetle　*Dermestes dimidiatus ab.rosea* Kusnezova　玫瑰皮蠹

S

saw-toothed grain beetle　*Oryzaephilus surinamensis* (Linnaeus)　锯谷盗

shiny spider beetle　*Mezium affine* Boieldieu　谷蛛甲

short angle sap beetle　*Omosita colon* (Linnaeus)　短角露尾甲

short hair spider beetle　*Ptinus sexpunctatus* Panzer　短毛蛛甲

Siberia beetle　*Dermestes sibiricus* Erichson　西伯利亚皮蠹

silverfish　*Ctenolepisma longicaudata* Escherich　灰衣鱼，蠹鱼，衣鱼

six spots spider beetle　*Ptinus exulans* Erichson　六点蛛甲

slender-horned flour beetle　*Gnathocerus maxillosus* (Fabricius)　细角谷盗

small-eyed flour beetle　*Palorus ratzeburgi* (Wissmann)　姬粉盗

small flour beetle　*Palorus cerylonoides* (Pascoe)　小粉盗

small sap beetle　*Carpophllus pilosellus* Motschulsky　小露尾甲

smooth spider beetle　*Gibbium aequinoctiale* Boieldieu　拟裸蛛甲

souring beetle　*Urophorus humeralis* (Fabricius)　隆肩露尾甲

Southeast Asia saw-toothed grain beetle　*Silvanoprus cephalotes* (Reitter)　东南亚锯谷盗

southern cowpea weevil　*Callosobruchus chinensis* (Linnaeus)　绿豆象

spider beetle　*Ptinus japonicus* Reitter　日本蛛甲；

Sphaericus gibboides (Boieldieu)　凸蛛甲

spotted hairy fungus beetle　*Mycetophagus quadriguttatus* Müller　四斑蕈甲，四纹蕈甲

spotty round beetle　*Anthrenus maculifer* Reitter　多斑圆皮蠹

squarenosed fungus beetle　*Lathridius minutus* (Linnaeus)　湿薪甲

storage spider beetle　*Tipnus unicolor* (Piller & Mitterpacher)　仓储蛛甲

stored derris root bostrychid　*Sinoxylon anale* Lesne　双齿长蠹

stored nut moth　*Aphomia gularis* (Zeller)　一点谷蛾

streak beetle　*Trogoderma teukton* Beal　条斑皮蠹

Surinam cockroach　*Pycnoscelus surinamensis* (Linnaeus)　蔗蠊

sweet potato weevil　*Cylas formicarius* (Fabricius)　甘薯小象甲

T

tamarind seed beetle　*Sitophilus linearis* (Herbst)　罗望子象

three-banded fur beetle　*Attagenus sinensis* Pic　三带毛皮蠹

tobacco beetle　*Lasioderma serricorne* (Fabricius)　烟草甲，香烟甲虫，烟草窃蠹

tobacco moth　*Ephestia elutella* (Hübner)　烟草螟

tooth powderpost beetle　　*Lyctoxylon dentatum* (Pascoe)　　齿粉蠹

tropical tobacco moth　　*Setomorpha rutella* Zeller　　热带烟草螟

Turkish grain beetle　　*Cryptolestes turcicus* (Grouvelle)　　土耳其扁谷盗

two colors ball stick armour　　*Monotoma bicolor* Villa & Villa　　二色球棒甲

two-banded fungus beetle　　*Alphitophagus bifasciatus* (Say)　　二带黑菌虫

two-color bat beetle　　*Monotoma bicolor* Villa & Villa　　二色球棒甲

two-spotted sap beetle　　*Nitidula bipunctata* (Linnaeus)　　二纹露尾甲

V

varied carpet beetle　　*Anthrenus verbasci* (Linnaeus)　　小圆皮蠹，多变的地毯甲虫

velvet long horned beetle　　*Trichoferus campestris* (Faldermann)　　家茸天牛

vetch bruchid　　*Bruchus brachialis* Fåhraeus　　野豌豆象

Vodka beetle　　*Attagenus smirnovi* Zhantiev　　伏特加甲虫

W

warehouse beetle　　*Trogoderma variabile* Ballion　　花斑皮蠹

warehouse spider beetle　　*Tipnus unicolor* (Piller & Mitterpacher)　　仓储蛛甲

warehouse wood hister beetle　　*Dendrophilus xavieri* Marseul　　仓储木阎虫

West Africa seed beetle　　*Callosobruchus subinnotatus* (Pic)　　西非豆象

West Indian drywood termite　*Cryptotermes brevis* (Walker)　麻头堆砂白蚁

Western drywood termite　*Incisitermes minor* (Hagen)　西部干木白蚁, 干木切白蚁

western lyctus beetle　*Lyctus cavicollis* LeConte　美西粉蠹

wharf borer　*Nacerdes melanura* (Linnaeus)　黑尾拟天牛

white back beetle　*Dermestes dimidiatus* Steven　白背皮蠹

white-marked spider beetle　*Ptinus fur* (Linnaeus)　白斑蛛甲

white-shouldered housemoth　*Endrosis sarcitrella* (Linnaeus)　白肩家蛾

white spotted beetle　*Trogoderma megatomoides* Reitter　白斑皮蠹

wood-boring beetle　*Ptilineurus marmoratus* (Reitter)　大理窃蠹

woodworm　*Anobium punctatum* (De Geer)　木蠹虫, 家具甲虫

Y

yellow-brown sap beetle　*Haptoncus luteolus* (Erichson)　棉露尾甲

yellow mealworm beetle　*Tenebrio molitor* Linnaeus　黄粉虫

Yunnan spotted beetle　*Trogoderma yunnaeunsis* Zhang & Liu　云南斑皮蠹

Z

zebra-breasted fur beetle　*Attagenus suspiciosus* Solskij　斑胸毛皮蠹

（三）拉丁文学名检索

A

Acanthoscelides macrophthalmus (Schaeffer)　leucaena beetle　银合欢豆象

Acanthoscelides obtectus (Say)　bean weevil, bean seed beetle　菜豆象

Acheta domesticus (Linnaeus)　house cricket　家蟋蟀

Aglossa caprealis (Hübner)　lesser tabby　小斑螟

Aglossa dimidiata (Haworth)　black rice worm　米黑虫

Aglossa pinguinalis (Linnaeus)　larger tabby　大斑螟

Ahasverus advena (Waltl)　foregin grain beetle　米扁虫

Alphitobius diaperinus Panzer　lesser mealworm　黑菌虫

Alphitobius laevigatus (Panzer)　black fungus beetle　小菌虫

Alphitobius viator Mulsant & Godart　Africa brown fungus beetle, brown fungus beetle of Africa　非洲褐菌虫

Alphitophagus bifasciatus (Say)　two-banded fungus beetle　二带黑菌虫

Anchonoma xeraula Meyrick　grain worm　米淡墨虫，米织蛾

Anobium punctatum (De Geer)　furniture beetle　家具窃蠹；
　　　　　woodworm　木蠹虫，家具甲虫

Anoplophora glabripennis (Motschulsky)　Asian long-horned beetle　亚洲天牛

Anthicus floralis (Linnaeus)　ant-like beetle　谷蚁形甲

Anthrenocerus australis (Hope)　Australian carpet beetle　澳洲皮蠹

Anthrenus caucasicus Reitter　Caucasus round beetle　高加索圆皮蠹

Anthrenus coloratus Reitter　Asian carpet beetle　黄带圆皮蠹

Anthrenus flavidus Solskij　golden round beetle　金黄圆皮蠹

Anthrenus flavipes LeConte　furniture carpet beetle　丽黄圆皮蠹

Anthrenus fuscus Olivier　carpet beetle　黑圆皮蠹

Anthrenus maculifer Reitter　spotty round beetle　多斑圆皮蠹

Anthrenus museorum (Linnaeus)　museum beetle　标本圆皮蠹

Anthrenus picturatus Solskij　arrow spot round beetle　箭斑圆皮蠹

Anthrenus pimpinellae Fabricius　bird nest carpet beetle, panda carpet beetle　白带圆皮蠹

Anthrenus polonicus Mroczkowski　Polish round beetle　波兰圆皮蠹

Anthrenus sarnicus Mroczkowski　Guernsey carpet beetle　根西皮蠹，格恩西岛地毯甲虫

Anthrenus scrophulariae (Linnaeus)　common carpet beetle, buffalo carpet beetle　地毯圆皮蠹

Anthrenus sinensis Arrow　Chinese round beetle　中华圆皮蠹

Anthrenus verbasci (Linnaeus)　varied carpet beetle　小圆皮蠹，多变的地毯甲虫

Aphomia gularis (Zeller)　stored nut moth　一点谷蛾

Araecerus fasciculatus (De Geer)　coffee bean weevil　咖啡长角象（咖啡豆象）

Attagenus augustatus Ballion　inclined belt brown fur beetle　斜带褐毛皮蠹

Attagenus augustatus gobicola Frivaldszky　brown fur beetle　褐毛皮蠹

Attagenus birmanicus Arrow　Burmese fur beetle　缅甸毛皮蠹

Attagenus brunneus Faldermann　dark brown fur beetle　暗褐毛皮蠹

Attagenus insidiosus Halstead　East African fur beetle　东非毛皮蠹

Attagenus longipennis Pic　long-winged fur beetle　长翅毛皮蠹

Attagenus pellio (Linnaeus)　fur beetle, carpet beetle　二点地毯甲虫，二星毛皮蠹

Attagenus sinensis Pic　three-banded fur beetle　三带毛皮蠹

Attagenus smirnovi Zhantiev　Vodka beetle　伏特加甲虫；brown carpet beetle　斯氏毛皮蠹，棕色地毯甲虫

Attagenus suspiciosus Solskij　zebra-breasted fur beetle　斑胸毛皮蠹

Attagenus undulatus (Motschulsky)　ripple fur beetle　波纹毛皮蠹

Attagenus unicolor japonicus Reitter   black carpet beetle   黑毛皮蠹，黑皮蠹

Attagenus unicolor simulans Solskij   black carpet beetle   短角褐毛皮蠹

B

Blatta orientalis Linnaeus   oriental cockroach   东方蜚蠊，东方小蠊

Blattella germanica (Linnaeus)   German cockroach   德国小蠊

Brachymeria obscurata (Walker)   chalcid wasp   广大腿小蜂，黄大腿蜂

Bruchidius atrolineatus (Pic)   dark stripes seed beetle   暗条豆象

Bruchidius dorsalis (Fåhraeus)   Gleditsia sinensis seed beetle   皂荚豆象

Bruchidius incarnatus (Boheman)   Egyptian pea weevil   埃及豌豆象

Bruchidius trifolii (Motschulsky)   clover seed beetle   三叶草豆象

Bruchus affinis Fröelich   lesser pea weevil   扁豆象

Bruchus brachialis Fåhraeus   vetch bruchid   野豌豆象

Bruchus dentipes Baudi   dark spots seed beetle, black spotted weevil   黑斑豆象

Bruchus pisorum (Linnaeus)   pea weevil, pea beetle   豌豆象

C

Callosobruchus ademptus (Sharp)   kudzu seed beetle   野葛豆象

Callosobruchus analis (Fabricius)   graham bean weevil   鹰嘴豆象

Callosobruchus chinensis (Linnaeus)　Southern cowpea weevil, azuki seed beetle　绿豆象

Callosobruchus maculatus (Fabricius)　cowpea seed beetle, cowpea weevil　四纹豆象

Callosobruchus phaseoli (Gyllenhal)　dolichos seed beetle　灰豆象

Callosobruchus rhodesianus (Pic)　Rhodesian bean seed beetle　罗得西亚豆象

Callosobruchus subinnotatus (Pic)　West Africa seed beetle　西非豆象

Callosobruchus theobromae (Linnaeus)　cocoa seed beetle　可可豆象

Camponotus pennsylvanicus (De Geer)　black carpenter ant　木蚁，黑木蚁

Carcinops pumilio (Erichson)　poultryhouse pill beetle　黑矮甲阎虫

Carpophilus dimidiatus (Fabricius)　corn sap beetle　脊胸露尾甲

Carpophilus hemipterus (Linnaeus)　driedfruit beetle　酱曲露尾甲，黄斑露尾甲

Carpophilus marginellus Motschulsky　brownish sap beetle　大腋露尾甲

Carpophilus sexpustulatus (Fabricius)　long wings sap beetle　长翅露尾甲

Carpophllus pilosellus Motschulsky　small sap beetle　小露尾甲

Cartodere constricta (Gryllenhal)　plaster beetle　灰泥甲虫

Caulophilus oryzae (Gyllenhal)　broad-nosed grain weevil　阔鼻谷象

Chalcosoma atlas (Linnaeus)　Atlas beetle　印度大甲虫

Chlorophorus annularis (Fabricius)　　bamboo borer, bamboo longhorn beetle　　竹虎天牛

Coccotrypes dactyliperda (Fabricius)　　date stone beetle　　棕榈核小蠹

Coptotermes formosanus Shiraki　　oriental termite　　台湾乳白蚁，家白蚁

Cryptolestes cornutus Thomas & Zimmerman　　horn grain beetle　　角扁谷盗

Cryptolestes ferrugineus (Stephens)　　flat grain beetle, red-rust grain beetle　　锈赤扁谷盗

Cryptolestes klapperichi Lefkovitch　　flat grain beetle　　亚非扁谷盗

Cryptolestes pusillus (Schénherr)　　flat grain beetle　　长角扁谷盗

Cryptolestes turcicus (Grouvelle)　　flourmill beetle, Turkish grain beetle　　土耳其扁谷盗

Cryptophagus acutangulus Gyllenhal　　acute angled fungus beetle　　钩角隐食甲

Cryptophilus integer (Heer)　　pleasing fungus beetle　　褐簟甲

Cryptotermes brevis (Walker)　　West Indian drywood termite　　麻头堆砂白蚁

Ctenolepisma longicaudata Escherich　　silverfish　　灰衣鱼，蠹鱼，衣鱼

Cylas formicarius (Fabricius)　　sweet potato weevil　　甘薯小象甲

Cynaeus angustus (LeConte)　　larger black flour beetle　　大黑粉盗

D

Dendrophilus xavieri Marseul　warehouse wood hister beetle　仓储木阎虫

Dermestes ater De Geer　black larder beetle, incinerator beetle　钩纹皮蠹

Dermestes ater domesticus Germar　domestic black larder beetle　家庭钩纹皮蠹

Dermestes carnivorus Fabricius　hide beetle　肉食皮蠹

Dermestes coarctatus Harold　double belt beetle　双带皮蠹

Dermestes dimidiatus Steven　white back beetle　白背皮蠹

Dermestes dimidiatus ab.rosea Kusnezova　rose beetle　玫瑰皮蠹

Dermestes elegans Gebler　Central Asia beetle　中亚皮蠹

Dermestes frischii Kugelann　fringed larder beetle　拟白腹皮蠹

Dermestes lardarius Linnaeus　larder beetle　火腿皮蠹

Dermestes leechi Kalik　Indian beetle　印度皮蠹

Dermestes maculatus De Geer　hide beetle　白腹皮蠹

Dermestes nidum Arrow　Americana beetle　美洲皮蠹

Dermestes peruvianus　Peruvian hide beetle　秘鲁皮蠹

Dermestes sibiricus Erichson　Siberia beetle　西伯利亚皮蠹

Dermestes tessellatocollis Motschulsky　red fur beetle, reddish pubescent dried fish beetle　赤毛皮蠹, 赤毛鲞蠹

Dermestes undulatus Brahm   ripple beetle   波纹皮蠹

Dermestes vorax Motschulsky   red belt beetle   红带皮蠹

Dermestes vorax var. albofasciatus Matsumura & Yokoyama   light belt beetle   淡带皮蠹

Dienerella arga (Reitter)   big eyes beetle, bigeye beetle   大眼薪甲

Dienerella ruficollis (Marsham)   minute brown scavenger beetle   红颈薪甲

Dinoderus bifoveolatus (Wollaston)   auger beetle   双窝竹长蠹

Dinoderus brevis Horn   auger beetle   小竹长蠹

Dinoderus minutus (Fabricius)   bamboo borer   竹长蠹

E

Endrosis sarcitrella (Linnaeus)   white-shouldered housemoth   白肩家蛾

Ephestia cautella (Walker)   almond moth   粉斑螟

Ephestia elutella (Hübner)   tobacco moth   烟草螟

Ephestia kuehniella Zeller   Mediterranean flour moth   地中海螟

F

Falsogastrallus sauteri Pic   archives beetle   档案窃蠹

G

Gibbium aequinoctiale Boieldieu　　smooth spider beetle　　拟裸蛛甲

Gnathocerus cornutus (Fabricius)　　broad-horned flour beetle　　阔角谷盗

Gnathocerus maxillosus (Fabricius)　　slender-horned flour beetle　　细角谷盗

H

Haptoncus luteolus (Erichson)　　yellow-brown sap beetle　　棉露尾甲

Hofmannophil apseudospretella (Stainton)　　brown house moth　　褐家蛾，褐织蛾，拟衣蛾

Holoparamecus depressus Curtis　　flat beetle　　扁薪甲

Holoparamecus ellipticus Wollaston　　elliptica flat beetle　　椭圆扁薪甲

Holoparamecus signatus Wollaston　　head horn flat beetle　　头角扁薪甲

Hylotrupes bajulus (Linnaeus)　　European house borer　　家希天牛

Hypothenemus hampei (Ferrari)　　coffee berry borer　　咖啡果小蠹

I

Incisitermes minor (Hagen)　　Western drywood termite　　西部干木白蚁，干木切白蚁

K

Kytorhinus immixtus Motschulsky   caragana seed beetle   柠条豆象

L

Lasioderma serricorne (Fabricius)   cigarette beetle, cigar beetle, tobacco beetle   烟草甲，香烟甲虫，烟草窃蠹

Latheticus oryzae Waterhouse   long-headed flour beetle   长头谷盗

Lathredius bergrothi (Reitter)   ridge winged fungus beetle   四行薪甲

Lathridius minutus (Linnaeus)   squarenosed fungus beetle   湿薪甲

Liposcelis bostrychophila Badonnel   booklouse   嗜卷书虱

Liposcelis decolor (Pearman)=*Liposcelis simulans* Broadhead   book louse   无色书虱

Liposcelis pearmani Lienhard   book louse   皮氏书虱

Lophocateres pusillus (Klug)   bark-gnawing beetle   暹罗谷盗

Lyctoxylon dentatum (Pascoe)   tooth powderpost beetle   齿粉蠹

Lyctus africanus Lesne   Africa powderpost beetle   非洲粉蠹

Lyctus brunneus (Stephens)   brown powderpost beetle   褐粉蠹，竹褐粉蠹

Lyctus cavicollis LeConte   western lyctus beetle   美西粉蠹

Lyctus linearis (Goeze)   European lyctus beetle   栎粉蠹

Lyctus sinensis Lesne   Chinese powderpost beetle   中华粉蠹

M

Martianus dermestoides (Chevrolat)   drug darkling beetle   洋虫

Megatoma graeseri (Reitter)   four-streaked long beetle   四纹长皮蠹

Megatoma pubescens (Zetterstedt)   pilose long beetle   柔毛长皮蠹

Megatoma undata (Linnaeus)   carpet beetle   波纹长皮蠹

Mezioniptus impressicollis Pic   north-west spider beetle   西北蛛甲

Mezium affine Boieldieu   shiny spider beetle, northern spider beetle, hood spider beetle   谷蛛甲

Migneauxia orientalis Reitter   roriental beetle   东方薪甲

Minthea rugicollis (Walker)   powderpost beetle, hairy powder-post beetle   鳞毛粉蠹

Monomorium pharaonis (Linnaeus)   pharaoh ant   厨蚁

Monotoma bicolor Villa & Villa   two-color bat beetle, two colors ball stick armour   二色球棒甲

Murmidius ovalis (Beck)   Murmidius beetle   小圆虫

Mycetophagus quadriguttatus Müller   spotted hairy fungus beetle   四斑蕈甲，四纹蕈甲

N

Nacerdes melanuraw (Linnaeus)　wharf borer　黑尾拟天牛

Necrobia ruficollis (Fabricius)　red-shouldered ham beetle　赤颈郭公虫

Necrobia rufipes (De Geer)　red-legged ham beetle　赤足郭公虫

Necrobia violacea (Linnaeus)　black-legged ham beetle　青蓝郭公虫

Neostylopyga rhombifolia (Stoll)　harlequin cockroach　家蠊，家屋斑蠊

Nicobium castaneum (Olivier)　pubescent anobiid　浓毛窃蠹

Niptus hololeucus (Faldermann)　golden spider beetle　黄蛛甲，黄金蛛甲

Nitidula bipunctata (Linnaeus)　two-spotted sap beetle　二纹露尾甲

O

Omosita colon (Linnaeus)　short angle sap beetle　短角露尾甲

Opatrum sabulosum (Linnaeus)　darkling beetle　欧洲砂潜

Opetiopalpus sabulosus Motschulsky　red-chested ham beetle　赤胸郭公虫

Orphinus japonicus Arrow　Japanese bat beetle　日本球棒皮蠹

Oryzaephilus mercator (Fauvel)　merchant grain beetle　大眼锯谷盗

Oryzaephilus surinamensis (Linnaeus)　saw-toothed grain beetle　锯谷盗

P

Palorus cerylonoides (Pascoe)　small flour beetle　小粉盗

Palorus ratzeburgi (Wissmann)　small-eyed flour beetle　姬粉盗

Palorus subdepressus (Wollaston)　depressed flour beetle　亚扁粉盗

Paratrechina longicornis (Lattreille)　longhorn crazy ant　家褐蚁

Periplaneta americana (Linnaeus)　American cockroach　美洲大蠊

Periplaneta australasiae (Fabricius)　Australian cockroach　澳洲大蠊

Periplaneta brunnea Burmeister　brown cockroach, Southern brown cockroach　褐斑大蠊

Periplaneta emarginata Karny = *Periplaneta fuliginosa* (Serville)　smokeybrown cockroach　凹缘大蠊

Periplaneta japonica Karny　Japanese cockroach　日本大蠊

Pharaxonotha kirschii Reitter　Mexican grain beetle　谷拟叩甲

Platydema ruficorne (Stürm)　red-horned darkling beetle　红角拟步甲

Plodia interpunctella (Hübner)　Indian meal moth　印度谷螟，印度谷斑螟

Prostephanus truncatus (Horn)　larger grain beetle　大谷蠹

Pseudeurostus hilleri (Reitter)　brown spider beetle　褐蛛甲

Ptilineurus marmoratus (Reitter)　wood-boring beetle　大理窃蠹

Ptilinus pectinicornis (Linnaeus)　fan-bearing wood-borer　梳角细脉窃蠹

Ptinus clavipes Panzer   brown spider beetle   棕蛛甲

Ptinus exulans Erichson   six spots spider beetle   六点蛛甲

Ptinus fur (Linnaeus)   white-marked spider beetle   白斑蛛甲

Ptinus japonicus Reitter   spider beetle   日本蛛甲

Ptinus sexpunctatus Panzer   short hair spider beetle   短毛蛛甲

Ptinus tectus Boieldieu   Australian spider beetle   澳洲蛛甲

Ptinus villiger (Reitter)   hairy spider beetle   四纹蛛甲

Pycnoscelus surinamensis (Linnaeus)   Surinam cockroach   蔗蠊

Pyralis farinalis (Linnaeus)   meal moth   紫斑谷螟

R

Reesa vespulae (Milliron)   museum nuisance beetle   博物馆甲虫（里斯皮蠹）

Rhyzopertha dominica (Fabricius)   lesser grain borer   谷蠹

S

Setomorpha rutella Zeller   tropical tobacco moth   热带烟草螟

Silvanoprus cephalotes (Reitter)   Southeast Asia saw-toothed grain beetle   东南亚锯谷盗

Silvanus bidentatus (Fabricius)   flat bark beetle   双齿锯谷盗

Sinoxylon anale Lesne   stored derris root bostrychid   双齿长蠹

Sitophilus granarius (Linnaeus)   granary seed beetle   谷象

Sitophilus linearis (Herbst)   tamarind seed beetle   罗望子象

Sitophilus oryzae (Linnaeus)   rice weevil   米象

Sitophilus zeamais Motschulsky   maize seed weevil   玉米象

Sitotroga cerealella (Olivier)   Angoumois grain moth   麦蛾

Sphaericus gibboides (Boieldieu)   spider beetle   凸蛛甲

Stegobium paniceum (Linnaeus)   drugstore beetle, biscuit beetle, bread beetle   药材甲，药材甲虫，饼干甲虫

Stromatium longicorne (Newman)   house longhorn beetle   家天牛

Supella longipalpa (Fabricius)   brownbanded cockroach   褐带皮蠊

T

Tenebrio molitor Linnaeus   yellow mealworm beetle   黄粉虫

Tenebrio obscurus Fabricius   dark mealworm   黑粉虫

Tenebroides mauritanicus (Linnaeus)   cadelle beetle   大谷盗

Thaneroclerus buqueti (Lefebvre)   clerid beetle   暗褐郭公虫

Thermobia domestica (Packard)   firebrat   家衣鱼

Thorictodes heydeni Reitter   carpet beetle   小圆胸皮蠹

Thylodrias contractus Motschulsky   odd beetle   百怪皮蠹

Tineola biselliella (Hummel)　common clothes moth　幕谷蛾，幕衣蛾

Tipnus unicolor (Piller & Mitterpacher)　warehouse spider beetle, storage spider beetle　仓储蛛甲

Tribolium audax Halstead　American black flour beetle　美洲黑拟谷盗

Tribolium castaneum (Herbst)　red flour beetle　赤拟谷盗

Tribolium confusum Jacquelin du Val　confused flour beetle　杂拟谷盗

Tribolium destructor Uyttenboogaart　false black flour beetle　褐拟谷盗

Tribolium madens (Charpentier)　black flour beetle　黑拟谷盗

Trichoferus campestris (Faldermann)　velvet long horned beetle　家茸天牛

Trigonogenius globulum (Solier)　globular spider beetle　球蛛甲

Trinodes rufescens Reitter　long brown hair beetle　棕长毛皮蠹

Trogoderma angustum (Solier)　Berlin beetle　长斑皮蠹

Trogoderma anthrenoides (Sharp)　Mexican spotted beetle　墨西哥斑皮蠹

Trogoderma glabrum (Herbst)　glabrous cabinet beetle, colored cabinet beetle　黑斑皮蠹

Trogoderma granarium Everts　Khapra beetle　谷斑皮蠹

Trogoderma inclusum LeConte　larger cabinet beetle　肾斑皮蠹

Trogoderma megatomoides Reitter　white spotted beetle　白斑皮蠹

Trogoderma ornatum (Say)　ornat cabinet beetle　饰斑皮蠹

Trogoderma sternale Jayne　carpet beetle　胸斑皮蠹

Trogoderma teukton Beal　streak beetle　条斑皮蠹

Trogoderma variabile Ballion　warehouse beetle　花斑皮蠹

Trogoderma varium (Matsumura & Yokoyama)　japonicus spotted beetle　日本斑皮蠹

Trogoderma versicolor (Creutzer)　European larger cabinet beetle　拟肾斑皮蠹

Trogoderma yunnaeunsis Zhang & Liu　Yunnan spotted beetle　云南斑皮蠹

Trogoxylon aequale (Wollaston)　California powderpost beetle　加州粉蠹

Trogoxylon impressum (Comolli)　powderpost beetle　方胸粉蠹

U

Urophorus humeralis (Fabricius)　souring beetle　隆肩露尾甲

X

Xestobium rufovillosum (De Geer)　death watch beetle　报死窃蠹，盗窃甲虫

Xylocopa appendiculata Smith　Japanese carpenter bee　黄胸木蜂

Z

Zabrotes subfasciatus (Boheman)　Brazilian seed beetle　巴西豆象

附录二

相关专业词汇 *

A

Action threshold（**活动阈值**）：确定害虫情况已无法控制，需要立即采取预防措施的临界值。

Active ingredient（**有效成分**）：杀虫剂产品中能够杀死害虫的主要成分。有些产品含有两种或两种以上的有效成分。

Acute effect（**急性效应**）：任何生物体内的一种生理反应，导致在短期

---

* 本附录译自：Safe Pro Pest.Common Pest Control Words and Phrases the Pro's Use[Z]. https://safepropest.com/pests-con/,2018.
New York State IPM Program of Cornell University[Z].https://www.northeastipm.org/schools/common-ipm-terms/,2020.
Glossary of Terms—Pest Control[DB/OL].https://www.finetuneus.com/resources/pest-control/glossary-of-terms-pest/.
Definition of Terms[DB/OL].https://www.orkin.com/scienceeducation/pest_library.
Paul J.Bello.&ACE.&BCE.Enhance your industry vocabulary[Z].https://www.mypmp.net/2020/07/06/enhance-your-industry-vocabulary/,2020.

接触有毒化学品或物质期间迅速发展的严重症状。对于人体或动物体来说，急性效应的症状是危险和严重的，但通常会在接触停止后消退。

Acute toxicity（急性毒性）：人或动物因接触化学品在短时间内（通常少于96小时）产生的不良反应。与急性毒性相反的是慢性毒性，它与长期接触某种化合物导致的不良反应有关。

Aeration（通风换气）：对经过熏蒸的建筑物或容器进行通风的过程。这个过程必须由有执照的害虫控制操作员完成。

Aggregation（群聚）：昆虫的多个个体集合占据某一空间称为群聚。如目前已知蟑螂之间能通过散发聚集素进行群聚活动。

Allergen（过敏原）：可以引起过敏反应的物质，如花粉、某些食物、蟑螂粪便、宠物毛屑。当敏感个体的免疫系统识别出这些物质是外来的或危险的，可能会产生过敏反应。

Allergic reaction（过敏反应）：身体的防御或免疫系统对过敏原的过度反应。过敏反应包括荨麻疹、呼吸困难、打喷嚏、眼睛发痒和流泪、血压快速下降或失去意识。

Antenna（触角，触须）：昆虫、多足类动物或甲壳类动物头部成对的、灵活的、分段的感觉附属物之一。主要用作触觉器官。

Antimicrobial pesticide（抗菌剂）：一类用于杀死有害微生物，如病毒、细菌、藻类和原生动物的药剂。用于杀菌或消毒。

Arthropod（节肢动物）：节肢动物是一种无脊椎动物，具有外骨骼、分段的身体和有关节的附肢，如昆虫。

Asthma（哮喘）：通常由过敏引起的一种疾病，症状是持续呼吸困难、喘息、胸部紧缩、咳嗽和喘气发作。

Asthma trigger（哮喘诱发因子）：引起哮喘发作的过敏原和刺激物，包括花粉、霉菌、室内尘螨和蟑螂粉末。

Attractant（引诱剂）：用于诱捕害虫的物质，既可以监测害虫的数量，也可以减少害虫的数量。

B

Bait station（诱饵站）：用于容纳害虫的诱饵，通常放置在害虫喜欢用作庇护所的地方。

Beneficial organism（有益生物）：对人类有益的生物。如以害虫为食、可减少害虫数量的捕食性昆虫。

Best management practice（BMP，最佳管理措施）：以最小的负面影响来管理资源或环境的行动指南，如保护地表水免于农药污染。此外，持续使用预防措施以减少化学治理手段的使用。

Biochemical（生物化学品）：天然存在或与天然存在的物质相似的化

学物质，如激素、信息素和酶。生物化学品通过无毒、非致死的作用方式起到杀虫剂的作用，如破坏昆虫的交配方式，抑制生长或充当驱避剂。生物化学品是与环境兼容的，因此对于病虫害综合防治计划很重要。

Biological pesticide（生物杀虫剂）： 又称生物农药，是从生物活体（植物、真菌、细菌等）分离出来的，或是其他非人工合成的用于害虫治理的化学物质。

Botulism（肉毒杆菌中毒）： 食物中毒的一种形式，通常是由于摄入储存不当的食物或饮料所产生的毒素而引起的。

Broadcast（撒施）： 撒施杀虫剂是指采用喷雾或喷粉等方式大面积地施洒杀虫剂。与之相反的是点喷。点喷杀虫剂是更可控的施药方法，宜优选。

C

Carcinogen（致癌物）： 能够使人类或动物患癌的物质。疑似致癌物质是可能导致人类或动物患癌的物质。

Cercus（尾须）： 位于蟑螂等昆虫腹部端节背侧后部的一对须状物，它的表面附有多种特定的大小不等、形状不同的感觉毛，这种带毛的感觉结构被称为尾须。它在维持昆虫的生命活动中起重要作用。

Chitin（甲壳素）：昆虫的外骨骼是由一种叫做甲壳素的物质组成的。它与甲壳类动物（螃蟹、龙虾、虾等）壳中的物质相同。

Chitin synthesis inhibitor（甲壳素合成抑制剂）：某些害虫防治产品利用甲壳素合成抑制剂来控制昆虫的生长。

Chronic effect（慢性效应）：药物在生物体中引起的长时间缓慢发展或经常复发的不良反应。

Clean-out（清除）：旨在清除所有有害生物的一种处理方式，通常在项目启动之初就完成，并且需要多个团队成员才能完成该项工作。

Commensal（共生体）：亦称共栖，指不同物种间共处，一方对另一方不仅没有影响，反而有益，如啮齿动物与人类的关系。也有的称共生体是一种利用宿主内部或外部环境中提供的食物，而不与宿主建立密切联系的生物，例如不以其组织为食。

Compound eye（复眼）：由许多独立的视觉单元组成的眼睛。例如，昆虫就具有复眼，其复眼是由许多个单眼组成的。

Conducive condition（有利条件）：可以吸引有害生物并被其利用的条件。

Conjunctivitis（结膜炎）：眼睑内表面和眼球前部的黏膜发炎。

Contaminant（污染物）：区域中不应有的有害物质。

Conventional pesticide（传统杀虫剂）：传统杀虫剂是作为农药使用而人工合成的化学品，是预防、减少、杀灭或驱除任何害虫的合成化学品。该术语通常用于指化学杀虫剂的活性成分，不适用于生物杀虫剂。

Crack and crevice（裂缝和缝隙）：昆虫的栖息地通常是在结构内的裂缝和缝隙中。

Cryptococcosis（隐球菌症）：一种传染性疾病，由真菌新生隐球菌引起，其特征是在肺、皮下组织、关节，尤其是大脑中出现结节性病变或脓肿。

Cumulative risk（累积风险）：反复暴露于具有相似毒性风险的化学品中而产生的附加或累积效应。

D

Defoliating（脱叶，落叶）：包括杀死植物组织或人为地加速植物组织的干燥，伴有叶片脱落或者无叶片脱落。

Disinfectant（消毒剂）：一种破坏有害微生物生长的化学物质，但通常不会杀死细菌孢子。

Dose（剂量）：给定时间段内摄入体内的有毒物质的量。常用于监视人体接触有毒物质的程度。

Dust（粉剂）：研磨精细的干燥化学品的混合物，常用于杀虫剂。杀虫剂粉剂由少量活性成分和大量惰性成分混合而成，这些惰性成分通常为滑石粉或黏土。

E

Ecosystem（生态系统）：指在自然界的一定空间内，环境中的生物（植物、动物）和非生物（空气、水、矿物质、气候）构成的统一整体。生态系统的范围可大可小，相互交错。

Ecotone（生态交错区）：两个相邻生态群落之间的过渡区。在这里是指环境中的有害生物活动趋于增强的转变区域。

Ectoparasite（体外寄生虫）：一种可以在其寄主的体表上生活和觅食的寄生虫，如臭虫、跳蚤和虱子之类的害虫。

Efficacy（效能）：描述某个物件在完成工作或实现目标方面的效率。

Encephalitis（脑炎）：脑部组织发炎。

Endocrine disruption（内分泌破坏）：由某些化学物质引起的人类和野生生物的内分泌系统变化或破坏，这些变化会影响激素水平和功能。

Entry point（入口点）：害虫进入建筑物内的入口位置。识别昆虫进入点是 IPM 检查的内容之一。

Environmental Protection Agency（EPA，环境保护署）：美国联邦政府负责建立和监督农药法规的机构。

Environmentally responsible（环保）：杀虫剂的施用和其他有害生物管理工作都必须对环境负责。

F

Fecal deposit（粪便沉积物）：通过观察是否有动物的粪便沉积物或粪便来发现昆虫和其他有害生物的活动。

Filiform antennae（丝状触角）：丝状触角是昆虫（如蝗虫、蟋蟀）触角中的一种。这类触角长而细，仅基部两节稍粗大，鞭节由许多大小相似的小节相连成细丝状，向端部逐渐变细。

Fogging（雾化）：对整个空间进行消杀的一种方法。雾化是一种触杀法，仅能杀死接触到药物的昆虫或蜘蛛，不能穿透墙壁和包装物。

Food chain（食物链）：指生态系统中所有动物之间相互依赖，通过一系列吃与被吃的关系而建立的一种联系。

Food poisoning（食物中毒）：细菌毒素或其他来源的有毒产物引起的一种急性胃肠道疾病。

Forage trail（觅食路径）：蚂蚁和地下白蚁沿着觅食路径行进，该路径是由这类昆虫的信息素沉积而建立的。

Formulation（剂型）：剂型是杀虫剂配方的设计。杀虫剂由多种配方制成，供灭虫专业人员使用。这些剂型包括水溶性颗粒、液体、乳剂和微型胶囊等。

Fumigation（熏蒸）：利用可以杀死昆虫的化学气体，穿透被虫害的物体，而杀死昆虫的一种方法。

Fungi（真菌）：一类具真核、产孢的、无叶绿体的真核生物，包括酵母、霉菌，以及蘑菇等。

Fungicide（杀菌剂）：任何能够杀死真菌或抑制真菌孢子生长繁殖的物质。

G

Gallery（虫道）：害虫在木头内挖掘的坑道，使它们在木头表层下的活动不被发现。

Garbage（食品垃圾）：因处理、储存、包装、销售、制备、烹饪和提供食物而产生的食品废弃物。

Generalist（广适性生物）：可取食不同材质，并适宜在多种环境下生存的生物。例如，Generalist insect 是指适应性强的昆虫。

Geniculate antennae（膝状触角）：膝状触角为肘形，常见于蚂蚁。

Granule/Pellet（微粒/小丸）：一种低浓度的干燥农药剂型，颗粒略大于灰尘，可以直接使用。

Ground water（地下水）：在土地表层以下发现的水，通常赋存于多孔岩层。地下水是井水和泉水的来源，经常用于饮用。

Growth regulator（生长调节剂）：一种加速、减缓或改变昆虫/植物正常生长或繁殖的化学物质。

H

Habitat modification（生境改造）：改变或改造周围环境的过程。例如，通过减少或消除吸引与维持有害生物种群的食物、水、栖息处以及堵截其入口点等，以减少有害生物发生的可能。

Harborage（藏匿处）：昆虫藏匿的位置。例如，昆虫可能藏匿在某些物品的裂缝和缝隙中。

Hardware cloth（五金布）：五金布是一种孔径较小、方形且材质较厚重的硬金属筛网。它是由各种尺寸的金属丝交织而成的金属编织网，可用于防止有害生物（特别是脊椎动物，如老鼠）进入，一般安置在建筑物的通风口等有害生物可能的入口处。

Hazardous chemical（有害化学物质）：此类物质能够产生不利的物理影响（起火、爆炸等）或不利的健康影响（癌症、皮炎等）等。

Health assessment（健康评估）：在指定位置对可获取的现有的或潜在的健康风险数据的评估。

Herbicide（除草剂）：一种旨在抑制植物生长或杀死植物（如牧草或杂草）的农药。农民和牧场主使用的所有农药中，几乎70%是除草剂。

High Efficiency Particulate Air Vacuum Cleaner（HEPA，高效微粒空气真空吸尘器）：一种特殊的真空吸尘器，可以清除地板、窗台或地毯上很小的颗粒与灰尘，吸尘后的尘埃不会再次散布到空气中。

Host plant（寄主植物）：寄主植物是寄生物或者病原物赖以生存的植物，是为病菌或昆虫等生物提供生活环境的植物。

I

Illegal pesticide（非法农药）：指未注册或已注册但非法重新包装的农药。最好在商店而不要在跳蚤市场或互联网上购买农药产品，以防这类农药的标签更改，导致使用已过期的农药。

Incineration（焚烧）：通过可控的高温焚烧销毁固体、液体或气体废物。有害的有机化合物转化为灰分、二氧化碳和水。焚烧会破坏有机物，减少废物量，并使废物中可能包含的水或其他液体汽化。产生的残留灰烬可能包含一些有害物质，如从原始废物中浓缩的不可燃重金属。

Indoor air（室内空气）：居住结构内的空气。有时室内空气会因与室外新鲜空气缺乏交换，而使其洁净程度受到影响。例如，残留在室内的溶剂、烟雾、油漆、家具胶水、地毯垫料和其他合成化学物质经常会导致环境或健康问题。

Indoor Rodent Trap（IRT，室内啮齿动物陷阱）：指用于治理鼠害的室内陷阱。

Industrial waste（工业垃圾）：在工业生产中产生或消除的不需要的材料，并归为各种类别，如液体废料、污泥、固体废料和危险废料等。

Inert ingredient（惰性成分）：惰性成分为某些农药中的非"活性"成分，如水、石油馏分、滑石、玉米粉或肥皂。在讨论农药时，惰性成分不会攻击特定的害虫，但某些成分具有化学或生物活性，会导致人体健康和环境污染问题。

Infestation（侵染）：指有害生物大批出没、侵扰和蔓延。尽管有些虫害一时是看不到的，但其造成的损害（如咬伤）与活动迹象（如粪便）可证明它们曾经来过。

Insect（昆虫）：节肢动物门内的一类动物，具有几丁质的外骨骼，三段式的身体（头部、胸部和腹部），三对节足，复眼和一对触角。它们是地球上种类最丰富的动物之一，包括一百万种以上的物种，占所有已知生物的一半以上。

Insect growth regulator（昆虫生长调节剂）：某些有害生物防治产品可以通过使用昆虫生长调节剂来控制昆虫。

Insect Light Trap（ILT，昆虫光诱捕器）：又称诱虫灯，可以发射紫外线波长的光，这种紫外光人类看不见，但飞虫可以看到。将该设备安装在建筑物内部，可以捕捉飞行昆虫。当飞虫扑光时，将其捕获到诱虫灯的胶板上。

Insecticide（杀虫剂）：用于杀死或阻止昆虫生长的化学药剂。

Integrated Pest Management（IPM，病虫害综合防治）：一种基于生态系统的战略，其重点是通过生物控制、生境改变、栽培技术改进和抗性品种的使用等技术的综合使用，长期预防病虫害。IPM 要求，仅在监测表明需要使用农药后才可使用农药，并且以仅去除目标生物为目标进行处理。选择和使用害虫防治材料的方式时应尽量降低其对人类健康、利益和非目标生物及环境的风险。

Integument（外皮）：昆虫的外表面。

Internet of Things（IoT，物联网）：虽然在许多行业中都使用了该术语，但由于出现了有助于有害生物管理计划的电子设备和监控传感器，因此它在有害生物管理领域正成为流行语。

IPM Committee（有害生物综合治理委员会）：该组织可以持续处理害虫管理问题。该委员会应包括来自学校、社区等所有相关部门的代表，如行政人员、员工和家长。该委员会的作用是制定有害生物综合治理政策和计划，提供监督和决策，并汇总各有关方面的信息。

IPM Continuum（**有害生物综合治理策略连续体**）：有害生物治理策略应朝向低风险、长期预防和避免虫害方向发展。当有害生物即将达到无法接受的水平时，防治策略首先应侧重于监视和化学抑制，最后以平衡的系统结束，即通过最少的人为和生物干预，使有害生物保持在可接受的水平。

IPM Coordinator（**有害生物综合治理协调员，IPM 协调员**）：负责对学校或学校系统的有害生物的综合治理政策进行日常解释的学校员工。IPM 协调员不一定是虫害管理专业人员，但是是接受过 IPM 专门培训的决策者，能够给出较为专业的建议并选择行动方案。例如，IPM 协调员可以是设施管理者或环境管理者，而对于内部具有专业虫害管理程序的学校，IPM 协调员也可以是虫害管理者。

IPM Plan（**IPM 计划**）：一份书面文件，其中包含有关学校 IPM 计划的特定信息，如学校所有职员、父母、学生和其他社区成员的 IPM 角色，农药使用通知政策，关键害虫清单，活动阈值，基于风险的控制方案等级以及用于主要有害生物的预防/避免策略，学校设施的检查时间表，与外部承包商合作的政策，解决技术问题的资源清单，其他相关信息。IPM 计划为培训新员工（包括新上任管理人员和临时管理人员等）提供了出色的工具。该计划是一个"活的文件"，会随着可用的新信息而不断更新。IPM 计划通常以活页夹格式制定，以便可以轻松添加和更新信息。

IPM Policy（**IPM 政策**）：一份书面文件，阐明学校对 IPM 的承诺并确定 IPM 的总体目标。该文件会定期更新，并在实施 IPM 计划时用于指导决策。

Irritant（**刺激物**）：会刺激皮肤、眼睛或呼吸系统的物质，比如氯气、硝酸和各种农药。刺激物可因单次高水平暴露而造成急性影响，或因反复低水平暴露而造成慢性影响。

K

Key pest（**关键害虫**）：指那些经常导致不可接受的损害，因此通常需要采取控制措施的昆虫。昆虫是否定位为关键害虫，取决于人们为有害生物设定的活动阈值。例如，在对可见度要求很高的运动场上，地老虎可能是主要害虫；但在邻近草坪区域，地老虎的一般性危害是可以接受的，这时它就不属于关键害虫。

L

Leachate（**渗滤液**）：渗入垃圾堆中并从废物中吸收溶解的、悬浮的垃圾成分以及被微生物污染的液体。

Least-Toxic Alternative（**最低毒性替代品**）：指与用于相同目的的类似产品相比，对人类健康、动物和环境的危害风险最低的产品和服务。

Lethal Concentration 50（**LC50，致死中浓度**）：又称半致死浓度（半

数致死浓度），表示杀死50%防治对象的药剂浓度，国际单位为mg/L，生活中常用单位为ppm。致死中浓度是一种通过吸入引起急性毒性的常用量度。

Lethal Dose 50（LD50，半数致死剂量）：指在指定的时间内通过皮肤或口服给药可杀死50%的测试生物的毒物剂量。半数致死剂量越低，该化合物的毒性越大。

Licensee（被许可人）：指获得农业部许可的个人，并且是法律法规中的负责人。

Lowest Observed Adverse Effect Level（LOAEL，观察到的最低不良反应水平）：毒性研究中对健康产生不利影响的最低剂量。

M

Management unit（管理单元）：将建筑物或景观的各个部分划分为多个管理单元，可以更准确地响应特定位置的条件。例如，将学校草坪分为前后草坪两个管理单元，前草坪和后草坪可能具有不同的土壤类型、阴影和坡度等。通过分别对这些区域的土壤进行采样和测试，测试结果将更加精确且有更好的施肥效果。虫害监测也可以分别进行，并且前草坪宜设置较高的行动阈值，因为其外观比不可见的后草坪更为关键。

Material Safety Data Sheet（MSDS，材料安全数据表）：有关有害化学

物质或极度危险物质的印刷材料，包括这些物质的物理性质、对人员的危害、火灾和爆炸隐患、安全处理建议、健康影响、消防技术、反应活性和正确的处置方法。

Mating Disruption（交配干扰）：指通过在设施内部放置某些性信息素诱饵来干扰害虫交配，从而减少昆虫产卵量或幼虫数量。

Mechanical transmission（机械传播）：机械传播是病原体通过有害生物向人类环境的物理传输。

Metamorphosis（变态）：动物在出生后一段时间内经历极端迅速的身体变化的过程。昆虫通过变态的过程而发育。

Microbial pesticide（微生物农药）：杀死或抑制害虫的微生物。有时微生物可以简单地通过数量增加、耗尽有害生物的食物供应以及入侵有害生物的环境来消除有害生物。

Microorganism（微生物）：细菌、酵母、简单真菌、藻类、原生动物和其他许多尺寸微小的生物。

Mite（螨虫）：以植物、动物或储存的食物为食的八足动物（节肢动物）。

Miticide/Acaricide（除螨剂）：能杀死螨虫的化学试剂。

Mitigation（缓解措施）：减少不良影响的措施。

Molluscicide（除螺剂）：杀死蜗牛和蛞蝓的杀虫剂。

Monitor（监控器）：用来捕获啮齿动物或昆虫的胶板通常是最常用的监控器。

Monitoring（监测）：指用以确定存在何种有害生物及有害生物位置和种群数量的一种方法。可通过人工检查、信息素和食物诱饵、跟踪粉末、机械捕获器和必要的胶合板来监控害虫。

Morbidity（发病率）：疾病的发生比率。

Mortality（死亡率）：死亡的发生比率。

Mouthpart（口器）：口器是昆虫的嘴巴，担负着取食的重任。昆虫具有多种类型的口器，如咀嚼、刺吸、舔舐、虹吸和锉磨式口器。

Mutagenicity（诱变性）：某些化学物质具有的可导致生物体的遗传特征发生改变，以至于对后代造成永久影响的特性。

N

Nematicide（杀线虫剂）：杀死线虫（微小的蠕虫状生物）的农药。

No Observed Adverse Effect Level（NOAEL，无可观察到的不良影响水平）或 No Observed Effect Level（NOEL，无可观察到的影响水平）：

不会造成可观察到的伤害的暴露水平。

Nocturnal（夜行性）：指一种动物行为。具有夜行性的动物喜欢昼伏夜出，在夜间很活跃，如蟑螂、浣熊和老鼠等。

Nonpoint source（非点源）：与明确排放点无关的任何污染源，包括雨水，来自农田、工业场地、停车场和木材作业中的径流，以及从管道和设备中逸出的气体。

Nontarget organism（非目标生物）：受控制措施影响但不是预期目标的生物。

Nutrient（营养素）：滋养和维持生命所需的物质。饮食中若缺乏适当的营养，会导致动植物健康受影响。

Nymph（若虫）：不完全变态的昆虫在发育过程中会经历三个阶段（卵、若虫和成虫），若虫是指未到成熟阶段的不完全变态昆虫。

O

Odor threshold（气味阈值）：气味阈值是大多数测试对象可以被检测和识别到的特征气味的最低浓度，即一种物质在空气中可被闻到的最低浓度。

Organism（生物体）：任何被视为实体的个体生命，无论是植物、哺乳动物、鸟类、昆虫、爬行动物、鱼类、甲壳类动物、水生或河口动物还是细菌，都属于生物体。

Outbreak（暴发）：就食源性疾病而言，暴发是指两个或两个以上生物体在食用相同食物后出现相同的疾病、症状或反应。

P

Palp/Palpus（触须或触角）：甲壳类动物和昆虫口器中的感觉附属器官。许多昆虫都用该外部感觉器官来品尝食物，如蟑螂。

Parasite（寄生物）：生活在另一生物上或内部的生物。寄生物会从宿主身上获取食物和庇护所，并可能释放对宿主有害的毒素或其他物质。

Pathogen（病原体）：引起疾病的生物实体。蟑螂和某些其他害虫可能将引起疾病的病原体运送或传播给人类或宠物。

Permeability（渗透性）：水或其他流体通过某种物质的难易程度。

Personal Protective Equipment (PPE，个人防护设备)：供工作人员佩戴或使用的专门服装和设备，以尽量减少人与农药或农药残留物的接触，包括耐化学腐蚀的衣服、手套、围裙、头饰和鞋类等。

Pest（有害生物）：破坏或干扰田地、果园、景观或荒野中正常的植物或者破坏房屋及其他建筑物的生物。有害生物还包括影响人类或动物健康的生物。害虫可能传播疾病，也可能只是滋扰。有害生物可以是有害的植物（杂草）、脊椎动物（鸟类、啮齿动物或其他哺乳动物）、无脊椎动物（昆虫、壁虱、螨虫或蜗牛）、线虫，引起或导致疾病的病原体（细菌、病毒或真菌），也可以是其他可能会损害水质、动物生存或生态系统的有害的生物体。

Pest Control Operator（PCO，害虫防治人员）：为害虫防治提供实际服务的人员。

Pest Management Professional（PMP，专业有害生物管理）：对影响城市人居环境的有害生物孳生的诸因素进行改造的管理模式。

Pest manager（害虫管理员）：指导他人在虫害现场控制有害生物的专业人员。害虫管理员必须接受害虫管理与 IPM 的教育或培训。

Pesticide（杀虫剂，农药）：用于预防、消灭、驱除或减少任何害虫的任何物质或物质混合物。

Pesticide residue（农药残留）：农药在处理过的物品中留下的痕迹被称为残留物。它是使用农药后，尚未被分解而残留于生物体、收获物、土壤、水体和大气中的微量农药原体、有毒代谢物、降解物和杂质的总称。

Pesticide usage（农药用量）：指农药的实际用量，通常以施用量或处理单位表示。

Pest-vulnerable area（**PVA，易受有害生物攻击的区域**）：在户内，易受有害生物攻击的区域是指有害生物可能进入或藏匿的区域。

pH（**hydrogen ion concentration 氢离子浓度指数**）：表示氢离子浓度的一种方法。它是水溶液中氢离子浓度（活度）的常用对数的负值，即 $-\lg[H^+]$。常用于表示化学溶液的酸性或碱性的量度，范围是 0 ~ 14。中性物质的 pH 值为 7，酸性物质的 pH 值小于 7，碱性物质的 pH 值大于 7。

Pheromone（**信息素**）：动物用于各种目的的化学信号称为信息素。

Pheromone Trap（**信息素陷阱**）：信息素陷阱是一种害虫控制工具，用于帮助监测和控制虫害。信息素陷阱通常由一个充满性信息素的胶水陷阱组成，雄性害虫为了交配被吸引到诱捕器，然后被捕获。

Plague（**鼠疫**）：鼠疫是由鼠疫杆菌引起的自然疫源性烈性传染病，也叫黑死病。它是通过鼠蚤传播给人类。

Point source（**点源**）：一个可识别的单一的固定位置或固定设施（如烟囱或废水处理厂等），污染物从该源排出或散发。

Pollution（**污染**）：污染是将有害物质引入环境，这些有害物质被称为污染物。任何物质（固体、液体或气体）或任何形式的能量（如热量、声音或放射性）以超过其以某种无害形式分散、稀释、分解、回收或储存的速度添加到环境中都会造成污染。污染物的存在通常会削弱自然资源的可用性。污染物的主要类别（通常按环境要素分类）有空气污染、水污染和土地污染。

Potable water（饮用水）：可以安全饮用的原水或处理过的水。

Power spray（动力喷雾）：使用安装在卡车上的动力设备将液体向外扩散的一种设备处理方式。可以输送大量化学药品。

Predator（捕食者）：捕食或狩猎其他生物以维持其生命的生物。

Pronotal shield（前胸背板）：德国蟑螂等昆虫可通过前胸背板上存在的两个纵向条纹来识别。

R

Recycling（回收）：重复使用原始的或已更改形式的材料和物品，而不是将其作为废物丢弃。

Reduced-risk pesticide（低风险的农药）：低风险的农药对人类健康的风险低，对非目标生物的风险低，污染有价值物品或者环境资源的可能性低，可扩大 IPM 的采用或使其更加有效。它可以是风险较低的常规农药，也可以是具有独特作用方式、使用量少、毒性低、目标物种特异性或自然产生的生物农药。

Reference dose（RfD，参考剂量）：指人类群体（包括敏感亚群体）在一生中可能没有明显有害影响风险的每日暴露量的估计值，也可以指可接受的每日摄入量的标准。

Release（**释放**）：任何向环境泄漏、泵送、倾倒、排放、排空、注入、浸出或处置危险或极危险化学物质的行为。

Repellant（**驱避剂**）：可用于驱赶昆虫或其他有害生物的的任何化学物质。

Residual（**残留**）：农药在施用后残留的产品或物质，有些农药可持续存留数小时或更长时间。

Restricted use pesticide（**限制使用的农药**）：只能出售给经过认证的施药者或只能由其使用的农药。

Risk（**风险**）：衡量可能对生命、健康、财产或环境造成破坏的可能性。风险被认为是农药毒性和暴露的结果。

Risk assessment（**风险评估**）：风险评估是一个系统的过程，包括识别、分析和控制危害与风险。包括识别可能造成损害的障碍和风险因素（危害识别），分析和评估与该危害相关的风险（风险分析和风险评价）。风险评估应由专业人员执行，以确定在任何潜在情况下，采取或应该采取哪些措施来消除或控制工作场所中的风险。

Risk communication（**风险交流**）：交换有关健康或环境风险的级别或重要性信息的过程。

Risk factor（风险因素）：风险因素是指增加风险或易感性的那些因素，尤其指与毒性作用机会增加相关的特征或变量。

Rodent（啮齿动物）：啮齿动物是最大的非飞行哺乳动物类群，其特征是上下颌有两个不断生长的门牙，必须通过啃咬来保持短小。啮齿动物包括小鼠、大鼠、仓鼠和通常作为宠物饲养的豚鼠等。

Rodent Bait Station（RBS，啮齿动物诱饵站）：啮齿动物诱饵站一般设置于设施外部四周，与设施相距为150至200英尺，目的是使啮齿动物在进入设施内部之前进食并在设施外面死亡。

Rodenticide（灭鼠药）：一种旨在杀死大鼠、小鼠和其他啮齿动物的农药。

Route of exposure（接触途径）：化学品接触后进入生物体的方式。如摄入、吸入或皮肤吸收。

S

Safety Data Sheet（SDS，安全数据表）：安全数据表曾被称为材料安全数据表（MSDS），它是一个文档，提供有关危险化学品的特性以及它们如何影响工作场所的健康与安全的信息，包括化学品的标识，健康危害，处理和储存程序，处置指南和应急程序等。

Salmonellosis（沙门氏菌病）：这种疾病可通过未煮熟或未加工的家禽

产品和鸡蛋以及含有未煮熟或未加工的鸡蛋的产品（即蛋黄酱）传播。沙门氏菌通常通过受啮齿动物或昆虫粪便污染的食物传播。

Scientific fact（科学事实）：科学事实是经过研究、探索等方法看到或找到前人没有看到和找到的科学事物，需要依靠科学事实，而不是观点。

Scouting（搜索，监查）：为了发现有害生物或有害生物破坏迹象，对藏品或建筑物进行定期的检查与管理。

Secondary pest（次生害虫）：与目标有害生物关联，或由于目标有害生物的存在而引起的一类有害生物。次生有害生物包括跳蚤、皮蠹及苍蝇等。

Source reduction（节源）：节源也称废物预防，是指从源头上减少进入"废物流"或以其他方式释放到环境中的有害物质或污染物的量的所有做法。它要求在设计、制造、购买或使用材料（如产品和包装）时减少垃圾产生的量或毒性。节源可降低回收、市政收集、填埋和燃烧的成本，有助于减少废物处理工作量和节约处理费用。节源可以节省资源，并减少污染。

Spiracle（气门）：昆虫或其他节肢动物的气管系的外呼吸孔，蜘蛛纲动物肺囊的通气孔。

Spray adjuvant（喷雾助剂）：任何自身具有或不具有毒性的湿润剂、铺展剂、附着剂、黏合剂、乳化剂、抗絮凝剂、水改性剂或其他类似试剂。它与农药一起使用时有助于施用或提高效果，并且须与农药分开销售。

Stage of development（发育阶段）：在变态过程中，昆虫会经历发育的各个阶段，这些阶段包括卵、幼虫（若虫）、蛹、成虫等。

Standard Operating Procedure（SOP，标准操作程序）：详细的书面说明，以实现特定功能的性能统一。

Surface water（地表水）：所有与大气自然接触的水（如河流、湖泊、水库、池、溪流、海洋和河口），以及所有受地表水直接影响的泉水、井水等。

Surfactant（表面活性剂）：促进起泡的洗涤剂混合物。

Synanthropic（近宅的）：对生活在人类居住区表现出偏爱的野生动物物种（如昆虫、啮齿动物和鸟类）的特性。

Synergism（协同作用）：两种或多种生物共同作用产生的总结果大于其独立作用之和；化学物质或肌肉之间的协同增效，彼此之间的效能会超出个体的单独作用。

T

Target pest（目标有害生物）：要成功进行有害生物管理，需要考虑目标有害生物的生物特性和行为，以使所采用的方法在昆虫学上是合理的。

Tarsus（昆虫的跗节）：跗节是昆虫腿部的最后一个部分，也是离身体最远的部分。很多昆虫的跗节及悬垫表面都生有一些感觉器官，可以感觉到接触物的情况，昆虫凭借这种感觉来决定其行动。

Thigmotropic（向触性）：向触性是有机体与固体接触后向某一特定方向的运动或生长。昆虫的向触性，表现之一就是它们更喜欢隐藏在可以紧贴它们身体的裂缝和缝隙中。

Third party audit（第三方审核）：第三方审核就是由双方当事人以外的第三方来监督管理，这类审核由外部公司执行。

Threshold level（阈级，临界值，临阈级）：在实施害虫控制措施之前，可以容忍的最大害虫数量。

Threshold Limit Value（TLV，阈限值）：阈限值是美国政府工业卫生学家委员会（ACGIH）推荐的生产车间空气中有害物质的职业接触限值。阈限值是指7~8个小时工作日，每周40小时内所接触有害物质的平均浓度值。

Toxic substance（有毒物质）：有毒物质是对生物有毒的物质，它是可能导致疾病、死亡或先天缺陷的化学物质或混合物。许多有毒物质是环境中的污染物，造成有害影响的量可能有很大不同。

Toxicity（毒性）：化学物质通过机械以外的方式对生物造成伤害的能力。毒性分为急性毒性与慢性毒性。急性毒性是单次接触后发生的中毒（接触后不久即产生影响）。慢性毒性是长期或反复的低水平接触有毒物质的影响（癌症、肝损伤、生殖失调等）。

Toxicity testing（毒性测试）： 毒性测试是对一种制剂可能产生的毒性作用的系统评估，通常是用无脊椎动物、鱼类或小型哺乳动物进行的测试，以确定某种化学品或流出物的不利影响。

Toxoplasmosis（弓形虫病）： 鸟类、人类和其他哺乳动物受弓形虫感染而导致的一种传染病。

Transition area/zone（过渡区域 / 过渡区）： 一种生态系统与另一种生态系统之间的区域称为过渡区域。

Translocation（转移，传送）： 病原体可能随其他材料或害虫被传送。

Trophallaxis（交哺）： 某些种类的昆虫，如地下白蚁，通过一种被称为交哺的行为来分享食物，这种行为可以是口对口的，也可以是后肠对口的。

V

Vapor（蒸气）： 液态物质蒸发或沸腾后所产生的气态物质。

Vent（排气口）： 气体排出设备的接口和管道。

Volatile（挥发性）： 是指液态物质在低于沸点的温度条件下转化成气态

的能力，以及一些气体溶质从溶液中逸出的能力。

Volatile Organic Compound（VOC，挥发性有机化合物）：易蒸发到大气中的任何有机化合物。挥发性有机化合物对光化学烟雾和某些健康问题的产生有重要影响。

W

Water table（地下水位）：是指地下水面相对于基准面的高程。通常以绝对标高计算。

Weed（杂草）：指生长在有害人类生存和活动场地的植物，一般是非栽培的野生植物或对人类有碍的植物。

Worker protection standard（WPS，工人保护标准）：旨在减少由工人和操作员的职业暴露引起的疾病或伤害风险的标准，通常专门指杀虫剂的使用。必须清楚地理解并遵循工人保护标准，以减少或消除接触风险。

附录三

不同藏品的虫害及其消杀法 *

藏品类型	有害生物	解决方案 / 处理
自然史标本			
昆虫	根西皮蠹，格恩西岛地毯甲虫 -Guernsey carpet beetle (*Anthrenus sarnicus* Mroczkowski) 小圆皮蠹，多变的地毯甲虫 -varied carpet beetle (*Anthrenus verbasci*) 火腿皮蠹 -larder beetle (*Dermestes lardarius* Linnaeus) 烟草甲，香烟甲虫，烟草窃蠹 -cigarette beetle (*Lasiderma serricorne*)	低温处理 热处理 气调 – 除氧剂处理 气调 – 二氧化碳处理 气调 – 氮气 / 氩气处理

---

* 本附录译自：Safe Pro Pest.Common Pest Control Words and Phrases the Pro's Use[Z]. https://safepropest.com/pests-con/,2018.

New York State IPM Program of Cornell University[Z].https://www.northeastipm.org/schools/common-ipm-terms/,2020.

Glossary of Terms—Pest Control[DB/OL].https://www.finetuneus.com/resources/pest-control/glossary-of-terms-pest/.

Definition of Terms[DB/OL].https://www.orkin.com/scienceeducation/pest_library.

Paul J.Bello.&ACE.&BCE.Enhance your industry vocabulary[Z].https://www.mypmp.net/2020/07/06/enhance-your-industry-vocabulary/,2020.

续表

藏品类型	有害生物	解决方案/处理
	药材甲，药材甲虫，饼干甲虫 -drugstore beetle (*Stegobium paniceum*) 百怪皮蠹 -odd beetle (*Thylodrias contractus*) 杂拟谷盗 -confused flour beetle (*Tribolium confusum*) 花斑皮蠹 -warehouse beetle (*Trogoderma spp.*) 袋衣蛾 -webbing clothes moth (*Tineola bisselliella*) 书虱 - booklice (*Liposcelidae spp.*)	
干燥的生物标本	钩纹皮蠹 -black larder beetle (*Dermestes ater* De Geer) 火腿皮蠹 -larder beetle (*Dermestes lardarius* Linnaeus) 白腹皮蠹 - hide beetle (*Dermestes maculatus*) 赤足郭公虫 - red legged ham beetle (*Necrobia rufipes*) 药材甲，药材甲虫，饼干甲虫 -drugstore beetle (*Stegobium paniceum*) 百怪皮蠹 -odd beetle (*Thylodrias contractus*) 花斑皮蠹 -warehouse beetle (*Trogoderma spp.*)	低温处理 热处理 气调－除氧剂处理 气调－二氧化碳处理 气调－氮气/氩气处理
剥制动物标本和研究皮肤	钩纹皮蠹 - black larder beetle (*Dermestes ater* De Geer) 火腿皮蠹 -larder beetle (*Dermestes lardarius* Linnaeus) 白腹皮蠹 - hide beetle (*Dermestes maculatus*) 花斑皮蠹 - warehouse beetle (*Trogoderma spp.*) 袋衣蛾 - webbing clothes moth (*Tineola bisselliella*) 家鼠 - mouse (*Mus domesticus*)	低温处理 热处理 气调－除氧剂处理 气调－二氧化碳处理 气调－氮气/氩气处理

续表

藏品类型	有害生物	解决方案/处理
	纤维素材料	
木材	家具窃蠹 - furniture beetle or woodworm (*Anobium punctatum*) 钩纹皮蠹 - black larder beetle (*Dermestes ater* De Geer) 粉蠹 - true powderpost beetle (*Lyctidae spp.*) 报死窃蠹，盗窃甲虫 - deathwatch beetle (*Xestobium rufovillosum*)	低温处理 热处理 气调 – 除氧剂处理 气调 – 二氧化碳处理 气调 – 氮气/氩气处理 视力检查 清洁用品
植物材料 （干燥的植物标本，篮子，树皮布，绳索）	烟草甲，香烟甲虫，烟草窃蠹 -cigarette beetle (*Lasiderma serricorne*) 粉蠹 - true powderpost beetle (*Lyctidae spp.*) 澳洲蛛甲 - spider beetle (*Ptinus tectus*) 药材甲，药材甲虫，饼干甲虫 -drugstore beetle (*Stegobium paniceum*) 杂拟谷盗 -confused flour beetle (*Tribolium confusum*)	低温处理 热处理 气调 – 除氧剂处理 气调 – 二氧化碳处理 气调 – 氮气/氩气处理 视力检查
纸，书，纸板	烟草甲，香烟甲虫，烟草窃蠹 -cigarette beetle (*Lasiderma serricorne*) 澳洲蛛甲 - spider beetle (*Ptinus tectus*) 衣鱼 - silverfish (*Lepisma saccharina*) 美洲小蠊 - American cockroach (*Perilaneta americana*)	低温处理 热处理 气调 – 除氧剂处理 气调 – 二氧化碳处理 气调 – 氮气/氩气处理 视力检查

续表

藏品类型	有害生物	解决方案/处理
植物源性纺织品（亚麻，麻，棉，绳等）	若此类制品加工过程中上浆，可能会遭到以下昆虫侵扰： 衣鱼 - silverfish (*Lepisma saccharina*) 家衣鱼 - firebrat (*Thermobia domestica*) 蟑螂 若此类制品有蛋白质类残留物，可能会遭到以下危害羊毛和皮革制品的昆虫侵扰： 袋衣蛾 - webbing clothes moth (*Tineola bisselliella*) 袋谷蛾，负袋衣蛾 - casemaking clothes moth (*Tinea pellionella*) 根西皮蠹，格恩西岛地毯甲虫 -Guernsey carpet beetle (*Anthrenus sarnicus* Mroczkowski) 小圆皮蠹，多变的地毯甲虫 - varied carpet beetle (*Anthrenus verbasci*) 百怪皮蠹 -odd beetle (*Thylodrias contractus*) 烟草甲，香烟甲虫，烟草窃蠹 -cigarette beetle (*Lasiderma serricorne*)	低温处理 热处理 气调－除氧剂处理 气调－二氧化碳处理 气调－氮气/氩气处理
蛋白质材料		
羊毛，羽毛，角，鹅毛笔，头发，毛皮，鲸须	根西皮蠹，格恩西岛地毯甲虫 -Guernsey carpet beetle (*Anthrenus sarnicus* Mroczkowski) 小圆皮蠹，多变的地毯甲虫 - varied carpet beetle (*Anthrenus verbasci*) 火腿皮蠹 -larder beetle (*Dermestes lardarius* Linnaeus) 澳洲蛛甲 - spider beetle (*Ptinus tectus*) 百怪皮蠹 -odd beetle (*Thylodrias contractus*) 袋衣蛾 - webbing clothes moth (*Tineola bisselliella*) 袋谷蛾，负袋衣蛾 - casemaking clothes moth (*Tinea pellionella*) 美洲小蠊 - American cockroach (*Perilaneta americana*)	低温处理 热处理 气调－除氧剂处理 气调－二氧化碳处理 气调－氮气/氩气处理

续表

藏品类型	有害生物	解决方案/处理
皮/皮革（和皮革胶水）/皮张，皮筋绳	根西皮蠹，格恩西岛地毯甲虫 -Guernsey carpet beetle (*Anthrenus sarnicus* Mroczkowski) 小圆皮蠹，多变的地毯甲虫 - varied carpet beetle (*Anthrenus verbasci*) 火腿皮蠹 - larder beetle (*Dermestes lardarius* Linnaeus) 白腹皮蠹 - hide beetle (*Dermestes maculatus*) 澳洲蛛甲 - spider beetle (*Ptinus tectus*) 药材甲，药材甲虫，饼干甲虫 - drugstore beetle (*Stegobium paniceum*) 花斑皮蠹 - warehouse beetle (*Trogoderma spp.*)	低温处理 气调－除氧剂处理 气调－二氧化碳处理 气调－氮气/氩气处理
羊毛和丝绸纺织品	火腿皮蠹 - larder beetle (*Dermestes lardarius* Linnaeus) 白腹皮蠹 - hide beetle (*Dermestes maculatus*) 小圆皮蠹，多变的地毯甲虫 - varied carpet beetle (*Anthrenus verbasci*) 烟草甲，香烟甲虫，烟草窃蠹 -cigarette beetle (*Lasiderma serricorne*) 百怪皮蠹 -odd beetle (*Thylodrias contractus*) 袋衣蛾 - webbing clothes moth (*Tineola bisselliella*) 袋谷蛾，负袋衣蛾 - casemaking clothes moth (*Tinea pellionella*)	低温处理 热处理 气调－除氧剂处理 气调－二氧化碳处理 气调－氮气/氩气处理
历史建筑的组成部分		
木结构	家具窃蠹 - furniture beetle or woodworm (*Anobium punctatum*) 火腿皮蠹 -larder beetle (*Dermestes lardarius* Linnaeus) 粉蠹 - true powderpost beetle (*Lyctidae spp.*) 报死窃蠹，盗窃甲虫 - deathwatch beetle (*Xestobium rufovillosum*) 黄胶散白蚁 - subterranean termite (*Retculitermes flavipes*) 木蚁、黑木蚁 - carpenter ant [*Camponotus pennsylvanicus* (De Geer)] 木蜂 - carpenter bee (*Xylocopa violacea*)	低温处理 热处理 气调－除氧剂处理 气调－二氧化碳处理 气调－氮气/氩气处理 视力检查

续表

藏品类型	有害生物	解决方案/处理
绝缘物品	美洲小蠊 - American cockroach (*Perilaneta americana*) 衣鱼 - silverfish (*Lepisma saccharina*) 书虱 - booklice (*Liposcelidae spp.*)	除湿（HVAC）
墙纸和胶粘剂	美洲小蠊 - American cockroach (*Perilaneta americana*) 衣鱼 - silverfish (*Lepisma saccharina*)	视力检查 清洁用品
石膏	米扁虫 - foreign grain beetle [*Ahasverus advena* (Waltl)] 薪甲科 - plaster beetle (*Latridiidae spp.*) 书虱 - booklice (*Liposcelidae spp.*)	除湿（HVAC）
木质地板和地板空隙	小圆皮蠹，多变的地毯甲虫 - varied carpet beetle (*Anthrenus verbasci*) 烟草甲，香烟甲虫，烟草窃蠹 - cigarette beetle (*Lasiderma serricorne*) 澳洲蛛甲 - spider beetle (*Ptinus tectus*) 药材甲，药材甲虫，饼干甲虫 - drugstore beetle (*Stegobium paniceum*) 褐家蛾，褐织蛾，拟家蛾 - brown house moth [*Hofmannophila psuedospretella* (Stainton)] 袋谷蛾，负袋衣蛾 - casemaking clothes moth (*Tinea pellionella*) 袋衣蛾 - webbing clothes moth (*Tineola bisselliella*)	视力检查 清洁用品 干燥粉尘
阁楼	家具窃蠹 - furniture beetle or woodworm (*Anobium punctatum*) 火腿皮蠹 - larder beetle (*Dermestes lardarius* Linnaeus) 粉蠹 - true powderpost beetle (*Lyctidae spp.*) 报死窃蠹，盗窃甲虫 - deathwatch beetle (*Xestobium rufovillosum*) 衣鱼 - silverfish (*Lepisma saccharina*) 褐家鼠 - Norway Rat (*Rattus norvegicus*) 蝙蝠 - Bat 鸟 - Bird (e.g. passer domesticus – house sparrow)	视力检查 清洁用品 干燥粉尘 除湿（HVAC）

续表

藏品类型	有害生物	解决方案/处理
美术材料		
画布上的绘画	通常不容易受到攻击	视力检查
木板上的绘画	家具窃蠹 - furniture beetle or woodworm (*Anobium punctatum*) 火腿皮蠹 -larder beetle (*Dermestes lardarius* Linnaeus) 粉蠹 - true powderpost beetle (*Lyctidae spp.*)	热处理 气调－除氧剂处理 气调－二氧化碳处理 气调－氮气/氩气处理 视力检查
纸上的绘画	烟草甲，香烟甲虫，烟草窃蠹 -cigarette beetle (*Lasiderma serricorne*) 澳洲蛛甲 - spider beetle (*Ptinus tectus*) 美洲小蠊 - American cockroach (*Perilaneta americana*) 衣鱼 - silverfish (*Lepisma saccharina*)	缺氧 视力检查
无机材料		
石头	通常不容易受到攻击；户外雕塑很容易受到鸽子和蝙蝠粪便的损害	视力检查 清洁
金属	通常不容易受到攻击；户外雕塑很容易受到鸽子和蝙蝠粪便的损害。另外松鼠咬铅	视力检查 清洁
陶瓷和玻璃	通常不容易受到攻击；可能会被一些小型飞行昆虫在表面留下污迹	视力检查 清洁

续表

藏品类型	有害生物	解决方案/处理
储存和运输组件		
非档案纸板，薄纸淀粉片	小圆皮蠹，多变的地毯甲虫 - varied carpet beetle (*Anthrenus verbasci*) 衣鱼 - silverfish (*Lepisma saccharina*) 家衣鱼 - firebrat (*Thermobia domestica*) 烟草甲，香烟甲虫，烟草窃蠹 -cigarette beetle (*Lasiderma serricorne*)	低温处理 热处理 气调－除氧剂处理 气调－二氧化碳处理 气调－氮气/氩气处理
新建筑构件		
胶合板绝缘	家具窃蠹 - furniture beetle or woodworm (*Anobium punctatum*) 火腿皮蠹 -larder beetle (*Dermestes lardarius* Linnaeus) 粉蠹 - true powderpost beetle (*Lyctidae spp.*) 报死窃蠹，盗窃甲虫 - deathwatch beetle (*Xestobium rufovillosum*)	低温处理 热处理 气调－除氧剂处理 气调－二氧化碳处理 气调－氮气/氩气处理

参考文献

本词典词条主要是从相关的英文文献中直接摘录，此外还参考了以下相关文献。

[1] 忻介六，夏松云.英汉昆虫俗名词汇[M].湖南人民出版社，1978.

[2] 李隆术，朱文炳.储藏物昆虫学[M].重庆出版社，2009.

[3] 张生芳，刘永平，武增强.中国储藏物甲虫[M].中国农业科技出版社，1998.

[4] Safe Pro Pest.Common Pest Control Words and Phrases the Pro's Use[Z]. https://safepropest.com/.

[5] New York State IPM Program of Cornell University[Z].https://www.northeastipm.org/schools/common-ipm-terms/, 2020.

[6] Glossary of Terms–Pest Control[DB/OL].https://www.finetuneus.com/resources/pest-control/glossary-of-terms-pest/.

[7] Definition of Terms[DB/OL].https://www.orkin.com/scienceeducation/pest_library.

[8] Paul J.Bello.&ACE.&BCE.Enhance Your Industry Vocabulary[Z]. https://www.mypmp.net/2020/07/06/enhance-your-industry-vocabulary/, 2020.

[9] The MuseumPests Working Group (MP-WG). Prevention–Assessing

Collection Vulnerabilty[J/OL]. [2019-10]. https://museumpests.net/prevention-introduction/prevention-assessing-collection-vulnerability/.

[10] Global Biodiversity Information Facility [DB/OL]. https://www.gbif.org/.

[11] NCBI Taxonomy Browser. [DB/OL]. https://www.ncbi.nlm.nih.gov/Taxonomy/Browser/wwwtax.cgi.

[12] Bug guide: Identification, Images, & Information For Insects, Spiders & Their Kin for the United States & Canada. [DB/OL]. https://bugguide.net/.